Paddling Michigan's Hidden Beauty

Doc Fletcher

Arbutus Press
Traverse City, Michigan

Paddling Michigan's Hidden Beauty: The Rivers, The Towns, The Taverns
© Doc Fletcher, 2012

ISBN 978-1-933926-39-1

Arbutus Press
Traverse City, Michigan
editor@arbutuspress.com
www.Arbutuspress.com

First Edition/ First Printing

Printed and bound in the United States of America

Maps © Maggie Meeker, 2012
Illustrations © Keith Jones, 2012, Bigtimeartguy, Inc.
Photos © Doc Fletcher, 2012

ACKNOWLEDGMENTS

Thanks to Maggie for making me laugh everyday. When you're with me, baby the skies will be blue, for all my life. Infinity Infinity.

Thanks to my eternally groovy family, for being eternally groovy.

Thanks to my friends for the smiles, hugs, love and the great stories.

Thanks to Michigan for providing me with enough fabulous rivers to fill another book.

Thanks to the ever-changing cast of my Crack Research Team for your contributions in laughs, stories and fellowship on the water, the details you uncover, the perspective you bring, and being there when you can.

Thanks to all of the wonderful paddling and environmental groups that we have here in Michigan, and the motivated people who make them run. Our state and its rivers are truly blessed to have you as residents.

Thanks to all of the livery owners, for your passion, for sharing your knowledge of the waters, and for making the rivers accessible to all of us. Special thanks to Leon and Tom at the Northland Outfitters livery in Germfask for making our Carp River trip possible.

Thanks to all of the fellow canoers and kayakers met along the way, for sharing you river stories, for your love of the rivers and for leaving them cleaner than when you arrived.

Thanks to the Quiet Water Symposium, libraries and nature centers across the state for letting me share my river experiences. Thanks to all of the folks who come out to our river talks - your attendance, excitement, stories and questions make it all fun.

Thanks to the WWII GIs for bringing pizza back home from Italy. Mama Mia!

Thanks to Verlen Kruger *("Never Before Never Again")* and Eric Sevaried *("Canoeing With The Cree")* for recording and sharing your incredible river adventures and in doing so inspiring us all.

Thanks to Susan Bays at Arbutus Press for your publishing expertise and for directing Maggie 'n me to Peegeo's.

Thanks to God for all the blessings that I've been given in Maggie, family, friends, and for allowing me to live my life in Michigan.

THE FIRST RIVER YOU PADDLE RUNS THROUGH THE REST OF YOUR LIFE. IT BUBBLES UP IN POOLS AND EDDIES TO REMIND YOU WHO YOU ARE.   -LYNN NOEL

CONTENTS

UPPER PENINSULA RIVERS

LOWER PENINSULA RIVERS

PREFACE

So many Michigan rivers, so little paddling time…

Thank you for (1) buying this book for yourself, or (2) thinking about buying this book for yourself, or (3) buying a copy for everyone you know, or (4) just flipping through this copy. *Paddling Michigan's Hidden Beauty* details day trips down 20 different Michigan rivers in both Upper and Lower Peninsula, some have lazy currents and some have fast water. All are rivers that are a short drive away: no matter where you live or visit in the Great Lakes State, you'll be within 2 hours of at least one of the 20 rivers.

This book was written as the complete guide to getting you on a river and to enjoy it with safety in mind. Along with my crack research team, I traveled down each of the 20 rivers with a camera, a digital voice recorder, and a GPS. The photos taken and details recorded share the experience with you and help you with the river trip, from planning to take-out.

Featured within each of the 20 river chapters…

1. A river day trip, usually 2 to 4 hours long. Miles and minutes are listed from the launch start to the take-out finish, and from the launch to key landmarks long the way. These landmarks act as your clock-on-the-water, letting you know how you're progressing against the total trip time/mileage.

2. The river's "degree of difficulty", to help match you and your group's paddling skills with the river's speed & challenges. Rivers are assigned 3 difficulty levels: Beginner is a good choice for your first canoe or kayak adventure, or for those looking for a nice, laid-back float. Intermediate is a river with twists and turns and/or obstructions that require some knowledge of how to steer a boat. Veteran a challenging river that requires precise steering ability.

3. The location of a canoe and kayak livery that can rent you boats and gear for that specific river, and help you with hauling and car spotting should you have your own boat.

4. A river map of the day trip.

5. A sign post that tells you how many driving miles it is to the river livery from 4 Michigan towns: Detroit, Grand Rapids, Mackinaw City, Christmas; and from Milwaukee, the home of Pabst Blue Ribbon beer.

You will also read about the history of a local community in the chapter's "Town" section. This section begins by locating your local Detroit Tiger radio station affiliate, so that you can follow the boys of summer while paddling away from home. Learn interesting history about the town, making the river experience that much more enjoyable. The chapter concludes by directing you to an old time tavern in that town, a place that serves a great bar burger and your drink of choice to go with it, making your great day on the river complete.

Each chapter tells the month that the river trip was taken. In general, this is helpful as the water levels will be higher in the spring, from spring rains and winter snow pack melt, and lower in the summer months. Higher water levels bring speed to a river, and trips taking 5 hours in the summer can take 3 hours in the spring. In general, the water flows faster in the spring and slower in the summer, so listing the month that the trip was taken in is useful information to gauge a river's speed. Please note that recent heavy rains will make a river fast, sometimes dangerously fast, during a day in any month of the year (safety is one of the benefits of talking to the local canoe/ kayak livery before paddling).

The 5-song musical soundtrack for each river trip is not available for purchase. Maybe someday. A soundtrack is included because music is one of the few joys in life that bring us as much delight as does time on the river. The songs selected for each river are in some way connected to the experience on that river, or in that town, or in the local pub, or simply because of how that song makes you smile or bop up and down. It's all bliss, from Roger Miller to the MC5.

To assist you in planning for your paddling adventures, this book includes a "Paddling & Camping Checklist" and a list of canoe & kayak liveries for rivers throughout Michigan.

I encourage you to visit our website, www.canoeingmichiganrivers.com. There you'll find ideas on different rivers to paddle, a calendar with upcoming river events including dates that we visit libraries and nature centers to talk about river adventures, a constantly updated list of canoe and kayak liveries in Michigan and in Wisconsin, a list of paddling and environmental groups across Michigan, and more.

The river quotes in each chapter run the gamut from funny to silly to reflective to thankful. I think the quote that best sums up the exhilaration that a day on the river brings was stated perfectly and succinctly by our Godson Spencer Vollmers, who said "We need to do this more often!"

Long may you paddle,
Doc Fletcher

DEDICATION

To Doug Killingbeck,

a hero who gave his life

to save a fellow paddler

Rivers in Michigan's Upper Peninsula

Carp

Indian

Menominee

Carp River
St. Ignace MI
Trip 6.4 miles/ 2 hours 12 minutes

Intermediate Ability

Livery: U.P. Wide Adventure Guide, W6508 Epoufette Bay Road, Naubinway MI 49762, (517) 899-6916, www.upwideadventureguide. com . Owner Kellie Nightlinger. Kellie asks that you call in advance for canoe or kayak rentals.

In addition to renting canoes and kayaks for Carp River trips, UPWAG offers guided experiences including Grand Island kayak tours, shipwreck snorkeling, fishing / hunting.

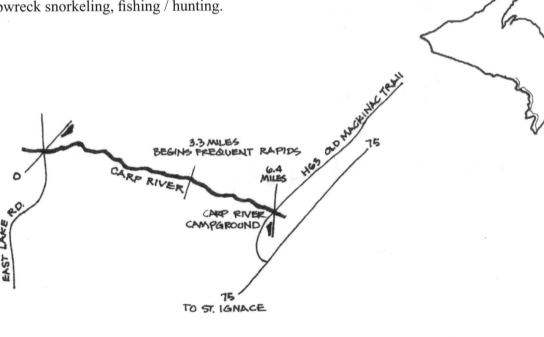

RIVER QUOTE...

Mister P: "One of the hardest rivers to get to, one of the nicest rivers to get on"

SOUNDTRACK: Kick Out The Jams – MC5, Born Free – Kid Rock, Memories Are Made of This – Dean Martin, Going Down – Jeff Beck, There's a Hole in the Bottom of tte Sea – Stewie Griffin

MILES FROM: 300 mi NW of Detroit, 239 mi NE of Grand Rapids, 8 mi North of Mackinaw City, 123 mi SE of Christmas, 367 mi NE of Milwaukee

Among our paddling group, it was unanimously agreed that the Carp was one of our top all-time river experiences. Although various sources described the Carp as one rated for beginners during the summer and fall (high water levels of spring requiring experienced paddlers), we found the river in early-July plentiful in both rapids and deadwood, and one offering a keen challenge to your paddling skills. Our experience was in what appeared to be "normal" summertime conditions, with no recent rains to affect the water levels.

This is not a beginner-friendly river due to many fallen trees and fast water runs encountered along the ride. To enjoy the Carp, your ability to steer a boat should be somewhat developed. There was no portaging required on our trip.

The beautiful, 45-mile long stream has its headwaters rising south of the town of Trout Lake. From there it meanders southeast, flowing through the Mackinac Wilderness until emptying into St. Martin Bay on the northern edge of Lake Huron, 8 driving miles north of St. Ignace.

The Carp is a federally-designated "Wild and Scenic River". Its final 25 miles is referred to as the *Carp River Canoe Trail*. It was within these last 25 miles that this chapter's 6.4 mile adventure took place.

The quote noting that the Carp is "One of the hardest rivers to get to, one of the nicest rivers to get on" refers to the difficulty in getting to the launch site of this fine river while using normally dependable maps, and in locating a good take out point that would allow us to exit the water just before the major logjam and the steep banks at the Carp River Campground Bridge.

Directions to the Carp River Campground and from the CRC to the suggested launch and take out sites…

To the Carp River Campground: from the St. Ignace intersection of US2 and I75, take I75 North to exit 352 (County Road 123). Turn right and drive one block on 123 to H63/Old Mackinac Trail. Turn left (north) on H63 and drive 5.2 miles to FR3445. Turn left and drive one-quarter mile to the campground.

To the East Lake Road launch access: from the Campground, go south on H63/Old Mackinac Trail for 3 miles to Charles Moran Road, turn right (west) to East Lake Road (East Lake Road is just before M123). At East Lake Road, turn right (north) & drive to the East Lake Rd access on the left (a few feet before crossing the Carp River).

To the take out site (3-4 minutes from the Campground): go north on H63/Old Mackinac Trail for about 200' to the first left-hand turn north of the Campground. Take the left-hand turn and follow it to the river. A few feet before the river, follow the trail to the right for 100' to where the path to the Carp is visible on your left.

     Carp River fishing includes brown, brook and rainbow trout. At the rivermouth ending near St. Martin Bay are steelhead and salmon.
     The Crack Researchers canoeing and kayaking the Carp in early-July were Mister P Pienta, Tom Kenney, Greg Palinsky, JJ Johnson, Dale Kittendorf, Nick Horbes, Chris Weaks, Ron Swiecki, Kenny Umphrey and Doc.

THE RIVER: PADDLING THE CARP

Launch northeast of St. Ignace at the East Lake Road access site. The directions are noted within the "Background" section of this chapter. On the section of the Carp outlined here, the river averages 2' to 3' deep and between 20' to 40' wide. You will paddle through frequent class 1 and class 2 rapids.

.2 mi/6 min: float beneath an iron bridge.

.5 mi/14 min: pass by the first of many enticing sandy points, this one as the river bends to the right. It's a fun test as you wind your way through a great deal of deadwood.

The river is very clean and clear. Its beautiful dark reddish-brown color is caused by tannic acid emitted from decaying leaves and other vegetation along the riverside.

.8 mi/20 min: on the right, a deep crevice cuts through the 8' tall bluff. Trees form a cooling canopy over you during much of your time on the Carp.

1 mi/26 min: as a Momma Merganser Duck and her baby swim by, a large tree fallen from the right shore blocks all but a 3' wide opening along the left bank.

1.2 mi/29 min: at a left river bend is a nice sandy break spot on the left shore, majestic birch trees are visible ahead; around the next bend is another sandy beach. 10 minutes downstream, the river is thick with deadfall and leaning trees, forcing the group to swerve left-right-left-right-etc.: *Challenge rating = mild; Fun rating = high!*

1.6 mi/40 min: a very small, clogged & active creek merges from the left.

2.7 mi/1 hour: on the tip of a peninsula as the river bends right is a fine sandy beach.

3.2 mi/1 hr 13 min: at a left bend in the river is a small beach on your left. Across the river on the right is a larger landing, with room enough for several boats. Take a break here to prep for the rapids ahead.

3.3 mi/1 hr 15 min: you begin to see very large rocks on the river floor, some up to 4' in diameter. 3 minutes downstream, rocks protrude above the Carp's surface as you enter into a burst of short rapids – a harbinger of things to come.

3.5 mi/1 hr 18 min: *you're into a wild and fast ride*, pinballing and maneuvering through a rock garden rapids – very challenging and fun!

3.8 mi/1 hr 24 min: at a left bend is a fine looking sandy beach on the right, the first in a series.

4.2 mi/1 hr 30 min: a sweet rapids run takes you winding along the rocks.

4.7 mi/1 hr 42 min: *"and they're off!"* You begin a fabulous 3 minutes stretch of swift current, twisting your way through the rock-infested rapids. Yee-ha!

5 miles/1 hr 47 min: a 100' long rapids precedes 2 large rocks, 4' in diameter and sitting back-to-back just right of midstream. They're poking their heads above the surface of the Carp, probably looking to see what all of the fun is about.

5.2 mi/1 hr 49 min: launch into a 6 minute long, real fine rapids run with a good deal of love taps and potential big thuds on and under your boat. A beauty, eh?

5.7 mi/1 hr 58 min: on your left at the base of a 5' tall bluff is a good looking break spot.

5.9 mi/2 hours: arrive at an impressively huge "permanent" logjam consisting of many fallen trees contributed by both river banks. A small angled gap in the middle of it all allows you room to maneuver through. Approach slowly.

For the first time in 45 minutes, the river returns to a sandy floor, free of rocks.

6.2 mi/2 hrs 7 min: on the left shore, a deep crevice cuts through the land.

6.4 miles/2 hours 12 minutes: you're in! 100' before the take-out, a creek flows into the Carp from the left, a promissory note letting you know that in seconds you will exit the river on the left shore, a few minutes upstream from the Carp River Campground Bridge.

THE TOWN: ST. IGNACE

Detroit Tigers local radio affiliate: WIDG 940AM

Father Jacques Marquette, a French Jesuit missionary, founded the European settlement of St. Ignace in 1671. The town was named by Marquette and his fellow Jesuits in honor of the founder of the Society of Jesus (i.e. the Jesuits), St. Ignatius Loyola. St. Ignace is considered to be the 2nd oldest settlement in the Midwest, behind only Sault Ste. Marie (est. in 1668). Until Detroit was founded in 1701, St. Ignace was the largest settlement in what was then considered "New France".

The 1671 St. Ignace landing by Father Marquette took place at East Moran Bay on the Lake Huron side of town, near a settlement of Odawa Native Americans (and directly across the street from where today is the Museum of Ojibwa Culture). Marquette's party arrived in birch bark canoes, the primary mode of transportation of the time. St. Ignace, positioned as it is on the northern edge of the Straits of Mackinac, the narrow connector of Lake Michigan and Lake Huron, became a key fur trading outpost. As the population here grew, so did the demand for birch bark canoes, creating a very profitable late-1600s business for the Odawa Native master craftsmen. The new St. Ignace residents were so enthralled by these canoes that many were purchased for use by family & friends back in France.

St. Ignace was the starting point of one of the great adventures in our history. In 1673, Father Marquette and the explorer Louis Jolliet were looking to find a water highway that would take people from the Upper Great Lakes to the Gulf of Mexico. In St. Ignace, their party launched two canoes into Lake Michigan and paddled west to Green Bay (the body of water, not where the Packers play); paddling south out of Green Bay, they rode against the current of Wisconsin's Fox River, taking the Fox to the 430-mile long Wisconsin River. Marquette and Jolliet canoed the Wisconsin River to its rivermouth ending near the town of Prairie du Chien in southwest Wisconsin where it flowed into the mighty Mississippi. Following the Mississippi River's current south, they reached the mouth of the Arkansas River, became the first Europeans to map the Mississippi River, and achieved their task of discovering an Upper Great Lakes to Gulf of Mexico water highway. Marquette and Jolliet's great canoeing round trip journey took them over 2,000 lake and river miles before returning safely to St. Ignace four months later.

West Moran Bay, on the Lake Michigan side of town, was home to a second settlement of Odawa Natives.

One interesting result of this culture clash was the difference in a dissolution of the wedded bliss: French women were not allowed to divorce; Native American women could show their man the door simply by putting his belongings out in the yard (*you were my wife, au revoir teepee life*).

Commercial fishing gradually replaced the fading fur trading industry as a way for St. Ignace residents to make a living. This came naturally to the Natives and the French, both skilled at fishing the local waters. They were soon joined by another group of highly skilled fishermen, Swedish immigrants. Lengthening the commercial fishing season was the invention of the ice breaker, introduced to the world by its St. Ignace creators in 1881.

In 1923, car ferries began to cross the Straits of Mackinac, transporting people and their autos between St. Ignace and the Lower Peninsula via Mackinaw City. These car ferries ceased to exist when the Mackinac Bridge began operations.

The Mackinac Bridge opened to traffic on November 1, 1957. The 5-mile long Big Mac is one of the longest suspension bridges in the world. For folks who love the

A well-worn trail connected the East Moran Bay Odawas with their West Moran Bay cousins. Between the two bays and just south of the Odawa trail, the New France folk built Fort de Buade to protect the budding fur trading business and the 60 new French homes. The fur trade brought the Native Americans (Odawa, Huron and Ojibwa) and the French together with a result that, today in St. Ignace, many residents are descended from either or both (6 of 10 St. Ignace school students are of Native American ancestry).

Late-1600s marriages between Native Americans and the French frequently took place without the blessing of a priest as the Jesuits took a dim view of such mergers. Marriage without a priest was known as a "country marriage" & the offspring of such a union were known as "Metis".

environs of the Upper Peninsula, very likely most people reading this book, the feeling that comes over you when cross the bridge northbound is a uniquely special one. A great Michigan tradition is the annual Mackinac Bridge Walk, held every Labor Day since 1958. The Walk allows people – frequently in excess of 50,000 - to walk the entire length of the bridge, starting in St. Ignace and ending in Mackinaw City.

There are fabulous views of the bridge from the *Father Marquette National Memorial* in St. Ignace. The Memorial is located on US2 just a few feet west of the southbound I75 entrance to the Mackinac Bridge (look for the small "Bridge View" sign on US2). Located on a high bluff overlooking the Bridge and the Mackinac Straits, the Father

Marquette Memorial conveys fascinating historical facts about the first meetings of the Great Lakes Indians and the French Explorers and has a fine Interpretive Trail Walk. The Memorial is underused and pleasantly, reverently, quiet – the perfect setting for the wilderness stories told within.

Area camping:

1) Carp River Campground, the end point of this chapter's river trip, provides you with a quiet and rustic setting. The campground features 44 wooded camping sites, each with a table and a fire ring. Call 877-444-6777. Campground directions are under "Background".

2) 8 miles south of the Carp River is the Straits State Park, home of the Father Marquette Memorial, at 720 Church St. in St. Ignace MI 49781, 800-447-2757. 275 campsites each have electricity, fire rings and picnic tables. There are four modern toilet buildings with showers and there is a playground. Fantastic views of the Mackinac Bridge are abundant from the campground and viewing platform.

THE TAVERN: TIMMY LEE'S PUB

"I would not <u>not</u> recommend this place", unusually strong praise for Timmy Lee's from crack research team member Ron.

We knew that we would like this place even before we saw it: from 5PM to 230AM, Wednesday through Saturday, Timmy Lee's offers a no charge shuttle from wherever you are in the St. Ignace area to the pub and back. If you're going to have a few beers there's no reason to not take advantage of this amenity.

The burgers are fresh pressed every morning, never frozen, with the ground beef brought in daily from the Pines Trading Post in town. The "Brokeback Burger" is described as "a hunk of beef between two firm buns". Not that there's anything wrong with that.

The fish is fresh, too, caught locally. Fish Fry Fridays features whitefish and perch. The whitefish dip is delicious with a kick, and the whitefish nibblets appetizer was a BIG favorite with our paddling connoisseurs.

Timmy's did a great job in crisping up the fries (a science not mastered by every bar). As Nick noted, "There's a whole crispy society out there". The 14" hand tossed pizza also received good reviews from the crack research team.

Timmy Lee's has ten flat screen TVs, video games, and a pool room. Just beyond the pool room is a door on the left, leading to the smoking patio, a nice place that gives you the feeling that you weren't just exiled outdoors. Every Saturday there is a band and every Friday a DJ. The entertainment included our hard workin' and feisty waitress Tammy, who gave it as good as she got it, and then some.

The juke box has an excellent selection of tunes. You don't often find Steppenwolf's "The Pusher" on a juke box. You don't often find Steppenwolf there, for that matter. Steppenwolf **and** the Zac Brown Band? Life IS good today!

The building that houses the tavern was built in 1947 and has had many different tavern owners. Before Timmy bought it in 2007, the pub was called "Miller's Camp" and had been moved to St. Ignace from Brevort where it was a tavern among a group of cabins. The original 1947 structure is the east half of today's bar (the half that is on your right as you walk in the door facing US2). In 2006, the west wing was added and remodeled in 2007 when Timmy bought the place.

A review of Timmy Lee's Pub wouldn't be complete without mentioning that every Wednesday is $1 bottled beer night, which includes a brand that is always a sure sign of quality, Pabst Blue Ribbon Beer.

Timmy Lee's Pub is located at W. 748 US2 in St. Ignace MI 49781, 1 mile west of I75 and 1/8th of a mile west of and across the street from the golf course. Phone (906) 643-8341. See www.timmyleepub.com.

Sources: Michilimackinac Historical Society, www.StIgnace.com, Father Marquette National Memorial, www.mackinacbridge.org, Tammy from Timmy Lee's

Indian River
Munising MI
Trip 5.3 miles/ 1 hour 54 minutes

Intermediate Ability

Livery: Kemosabe Cabins, 9215 Powell Lake Road, Munising/Wetmore MI 49895, (906) 387-4538, www. kemosabecabins.com. Owners Jeff Minch and Sherry Carros.

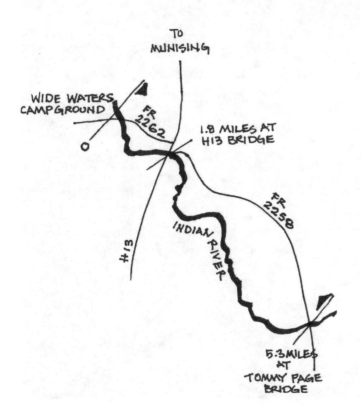

TO MUNISING

WIDE WATERS CAMPGROUND

FR 2262

1.8 MILES AT H13 BRIDGE

#13

FR 2258

INDIAN RIVER

5.3 MILES AT TOMMY PAGE BRIDGE

INDIAN

SOUNDTRACK:

Bottomless Lake – John Prine, Heaven For Me – Brian Flechsig & Charlie Weaver, Mexican Shuffle – Herb Alpert, The Piano Has Been Drinking (not me) – Tom Waits, I've Got My Mojo Working – Muddy Waters

RIVER QUOTES...

- Z-Bob 1990 flashback: "Ain't no hill for a climber"
- Bonus quote: "Reintarnation - coming back to life as a hillbilly"

MILES: 412 mi NW of Detroit, 350 mi North of Grand Rapids, 124 mi NW of Mackinaw City, 7 mi SE of Christmas, 288 mi NE of Milwaukee

THE BACKGROUND: INDIAN RIVER

The Indian River 5-mile long trip outlined in this book ends at the Tommy Page Bridge. Tommy Page (actual spelling of his last name was "Paige") lived and worked in the area during the logging days. During the late-1800s, the natural flow of the Indian River was interrupted by a series of dams. By opening and closing the dams, lumbermen floated their logs downstream. They would first pile logs along the banks while the dam backed up a deep and narrow pool of water. In the high-water springtime, the logs would be rolled into the river, and the boards blocking an opening in the dam would be

pulled, the flood would be released and careening downstream would go the logs.

One of these log and earth dams was built at the exact point of where the 5-mile trip exits the river, referred to as the "10 Mile Dam" (a dam long since removed). On the nearby flat ground was the 10 Mile Camp where the lumbermen lived. One of those lumbermen was Tommy Page. Tommy, as the camp cook and a colorful character, was very popular with the men (the unsurprising outcome when you feed people and make them laugh). After the camp closed in 1900, Tommy continued to live here, becoming the unofficial maintenance man of the lumber company buildings left behind. Due to his popularity and his efforts in maintaining the old lumber camp's buildings, the bridge just downstream from the dam became known as Tommy Page's Bridge.

The headwaters of the 40-mile long Indian River cascade down from Fish Lake, 15 miles south of Munising. From there, the Indian meanders southeast until it flows into Indian Lake near Manistique at the northern edge of Lake Michigan.

Taking a day trip down the Indian was suggested to us by Bill Duckwall (owner of Uncle Ducky Outfitters in Marquette), a man who knows the U.P. rivers as well as anyone I've met. If you act on Bill's Indian River tip, you won't go wrong. Several fast water runs, particularly above the H13 Bridge, and deadfall paddling challenges make for an exciting day on the water.

Kemosabe Cabins not only rents the canoes and kayaks, but their cabins make for great overnight lodging. Jeff and Sherry have 6 rental units. We rented two adjoining cabins for the 7 of us, giving us 4 bedrooms and a big living space and kitchen. Along with the very reasonable price, the gorgeous wooded surroundings of the Hiawatha Forest, an evening campfire complete with mouth-watering Navigator Pizza delivered (see "The Town" section) and it all made for a wonderful place to relax after a fine day on the river.

Directions to Kemosabe and to the Indian River launch and take out sites…

To Kemosabe Cabins: from Wetmore and the intersection of M28/M94 and H13, take H13 south for 5 miles. Turn right on to Powell Lake Road. Kemosabe Cabins will be on your left in one mile.

To the Widewaters launch site: from Kemosabe, take Powell Lake Road east (right) to H13, then south (right) for 7 miles to FR2262 (from the intersection of H13 and M28, take H13 south for 12 miles). Turn right (west) at FR2262. The access is one-half mile away.

To the Tommy Page take out site: from Widewaters, go south on H13 for only 50' to FR2258. Turn left (east) and drive 2 miles. After crossing the river turn right at the "Indian River Canoe Access/Pine Marten Run Trailhead" sign.

The Indian River offers excellent brown trout fishing along with brookies and rainbows and, from the river's source at Fish Lake, smallmouth bass.

Crack Researchers on the Carp in early-July were Mister P Pienta, Dale Kittendorf, Nick Horbes, Chris Weaks, Ron Swiecki, Kenny Umphrey and Doc.

THE RIVER: PADDLING THE INDIAN

From the first of two Widewaters' launch sites, and the one taken for this book, you look out from the boat ramp at 3 bodies of water. Each of the 3 is separated by a line of trees. From right to left, the incoming and narrow Indian River headwaters, Fish Lake, and the now widened (to over 100 yards) Indian River flowing to the left, which you will follow.

For most of the Indian River journey, the river is 20' to 40' wide at a depth of 1' to 3'. The exception to the 20' to 40' width occurs during the first 1 mile, about 30 minutes of paddling. During this 30 minutes, the river width yo-yos back and forth from its initial 300' to 30' a total of 3 times, as the river girdle alternates between loosening and tightening until it finally settles into the comfortable 30' width. Experiencing the football-field sized widenings makes it clear where Widewaters gets its name.

Over this initial half hour, tall pines are interspersed among the equally majestic birch trees. A wide band of lily pads appears among both banks and a bed of sea grass covers the river floor. On the left, you pass by the second of two Widewaters launch sites at the .8 mile mark.

1.1 mi/33 min: at the point where the final river narrowing takes place is a "permanent" logjam. Far left, a tiny gap allows passage. A great deal of deadfall is visible ahead.

The small gaps in the many Indian River deadwood fields will bounce you from the left bank to the right bank over and over. It's a very enjoyable paddling challenge, but not one well-suited to first-timers.

1.6 mi/44 min: *ya-hoo! A 6-minute long rapids run begins*, really nice whitewater that takes you all the way to the H13 Bridge.

1.8 mi/50 min: the absolutely wonderful rapids comes to an end as you paddle beneath the H13 Bridge. Beyond the bridge, you enter into a period of calm beauty floating by tall trees at the edge of both riverbanks.

2.1 mi/55 min: begin a fine 3-minute long stretch of class 1 rapids. As these rapids end you'll see 3 pilings sticking above the water line near the left bank.

2.4 mi/1 hour: pass among 4 tall rows of pilings stretched across the entire river, letting you know you're just beyond the half-way point of today's trip (under 1 hour remains).

3.4 mi/1 hr 30 min: a deep logjam provides you with a paddle opening to the far right; just downstream is a 30' long island passable right or left.

4 miles/1 hr 28 min: a home sits at the end of a short straightaway as the river bends left.

*Ron notes, "Mad Dog does not have a **'best if stupid by'** date".*

4.7 mi/1 hr 45 min: a "Lakes" sign is on the left; 1 minute downstream, a house is on the left shore hill.

5 miles/1 hr 49 min: at a river bend right is a midstream island, passable left or right.

5.3 miles/1 hour 54 minutes: you're in! The take out is on the right sloping bank. The Tommy Page Bridge is visible downstream.

THE TOWN: MUNISING

Detroit Tigers local radio affiliate: WDMJ 1320AM

Munising is located within Alger County, the town and county together named one of the Top Ten Destinations in the U.S. by www.virtualtourist.com. The Hiawatha National Forest… Grand Island… 17 waterfalls… Pictured Rocks National Shoreline… 260 lakes and 64 streams within 30 miles. The area is stunning in its beauty.

The Obijwa Native American tribe resided here for centuries before the arrival of the first Europeans. In the Ojibwa language, *Minis-ing* means "place of the Grand Island". Winter can be a bit long in this gorgeous land, & *Gitchi miigwech Gzhemnidoo gaawiin zookpog* is Ojibwa, or Chippewa, for "thank the creator it stopped snowing".

Due to an average annual snowfall of 230 inches plus concerted efforts to make sure the trails are well-groomed and well-marked, Munising and Alger County has become known as the "Snowmobile Capital of the Midwest". 300 miles of trails allow you to travel through as pristine an area as you'll find anywhere.

Five hundred million years ago, over 499 million years before personal floatation devices, much of the Alger County region was covered with a huge body of water called the Munising Sea. The shifting tides of the Munising Sea left deposits which created, among others works of art, Pictured Rocks. *The Pictured Rocks National Shoreline* is made up of 15 miles of shoreline along Lake Superior and features multi-colored sandstone cliffs that rise as tall as 200'. The view creates a special memory.

During the Ice Age, it is believed that up to 4 glaciers came into this area before receding. When the last glacier retreated 10,000 years ago, it left Lake Nipissing. Movements of that last glacier and Lake Nipissing formed the Grand Sable Dunes. The level of Lake Nipissing gradually receded 2,500 years ago, and what is left of this great glacial lake became known as Lake Superior. How big must Lake Nipissing have been to have Lake Superior as its remains? Crack researchers Vid and Jimmy would've been hard pressed to paddle across it.

Alger County and its coastline were well known to the early French explorers for many years while our continent's interior was still a vast, unknown wilderness. By the 1700s, maps printed in France located les Grandes Sable (the Grand Sable Dunes) and le Grand Marais, among the first North American names to appear on their maps.

Lake Superior near here was the starting point for European exploration of North America. The French followed a frequently used Native American water trail to take them from the Munising area south to Whitefish River on into Little

Bay De Noc to Green Bay at Escanaba. Out of the bottom of Green Bay, the explorers could follow Wisconsin rivers until they reached the Mississippi River, the key to opening up the continent's interior.

Sitting outdoors while having breakfast at a Munising restaurant, looking out at Lake Superior and Grand Island, you wonder why those French explorers ever left the area. They must have been dedicated to their work, because they were leaving a setting as pretty as you can imagine, with the sun dancing on the surface of the hypnotic blue of *Gitchie Gumee*, Ojibwa, or Gordon Lightfoot, for Lake Superior. Grand Island is just north of Munising out into the Big Lake. It is worth a visit and only a short ferry ride away. From its 300' tall cliffs, you have extraordinary views of Pictured Rocks. Grand Island offers plenty of hiking and biking trails and sea kayak tours of coves and rock formations. If after a day of exploration you'd like to stay overnight, the island has 17 designated campsites.

Munising is also a fun walkabout town. Stop in the Corktown's back room for a game of ping pong (very friendly regulars), grab a burger at the Log Jam (for more info, see "The Tavern" section) or browse at bit at the Falling Rock Café & Book Store. And then there was the pizza from "The Navigator" on Munising Avenue. After our day on the Indian River, The Navigator delivered pizzas to us at our Kemosabe Cabins, a good 12 miles away. Even after the 12 mile delivery, our crack research team found it to be some of the absolute best pizza they ever had – and very filling! They only make one size, 16", to simplify the ordering process. Call The Navigator at (906) 387-1555.

Area camping: the Indian River launch site at Widewaters is a good option. Widewaters has 34 camping sites each with a table and a grill. Drinking water pumps and vault toilets are located throughout the campground. Benches are placed at various spots for viewing along the river. Call (906) 387-2512 for details or reservations.

For more information on Munising and Alger County, go to www.munising.org.

THE TAVERN: LOG JAM BAR & GRILL

Ooooo – this burger is go-od!!!, the demonstrative, unanimous decision of Kenny, Mister P and me. Adding condiments to the Log Jam burgers would be a waste. The burgers and the fish here are fresh, never frozen, with the fish reported to be still kickin' as your meal is being prepared. If the burgers are indicative of the quality of the rest of the menu, the folks in Munising must eat here frequently (gotta try that whitefish and homemade pizza next time in town).

The sign behind the bar reads, "Everyone needs something to believe in - I believe I'll have another beer". It would be nice to have something to go along with that burger, after all. The word on the street is that Pabst is an excellent compliment to bar burgers.

If you like old time, feel good pubs, you'll like the Log Jam. Real nice bar, real nice folks. The look of the tavern grabs you as soon as you walk in.

The building was first a grocery store when it was built in the 1930s. When the grocery store was remodeled into a tavern in the 1940s, the gorgeous back bar (with a strong 1800s look about it), once part of a big ship, was brought in. The other half of this back bar piece is in place at the Harbor Inn Bar in Manistique.

A mural, including scenes from the logging days, stretches across all 4 walls. The mural was painted by the bar's original owner, Johnny Tervo. Looking down at it all from above is a tin ceiling that makes you feel as if it now was those long ago logging days.

The Log Jam has a picnic table and a patio out back for smokers or anyone who wants to sip their beers in the great outdoors. A pool table is inside if you'd like to shoot a game.

The tavern's tall, cool-looking tables were built by one of the Log Jam's regulars, Ole (pronounce it "all-e" when you say hi). Ole built footrests into the tables, but the paneling he wanted to include below the table top was vetoed by a friend who said, "you can't do that – it'll block the view of the ladies legs" (now you know the *rest* of the story). Ole's Mom was the first female to captain a 100-ton vessel out on Lake Superior.

The owner of the Log Jam is Denise Schlehuber. Denise was once an art teacher, later running an art studio/store before getting into the pub business - interesting livelihood transition. Before making the move to Munising and operating the Log Jam, Denise owned a bar in Moran near St. Ignace. Drawing (pun intended) on her background, Denise did some of the touch-ups on the Log Jam's wall mural. Real nice bar, real nice folks, real nice owner.

To reassure you that when you're in the Log Jam you're in a good place, right next door is Northwoods Home Nursing & Hospice. So, if drinking does age you prematurely, what better place to be?

The Log Jam Bar & Grill is located at 127 E. Superior Street in Munising MI 49862. Phone (906) 387-3737.

Sources: Munising Visitors Bureau, Great Lakes Life and Time Magazine (Ojibwa quotes), Alger County – A Centennial History 1885 to 1985, Munising Visitors Guide, 10 Mile Dam riverside marker, Lisa Cromell, Jeff Finch, Denise Schlehuber & Ole

MENOMINEE RIVER

Iron Mountain MI
Trip 5 miles
1 hour & 56 minutes

Beginner Ability

Livery: Northwoods Wilderness Outfitters, N4088 Pine Mountain Road at US2, Iron Mountain MI 49801, (906) 774-9009, www. northwoodoutfitters.com. Owners Randy (Gus) and Cindy Gustafson. Northwoods also services the Brule River, the Michigamme River and the Pine River.

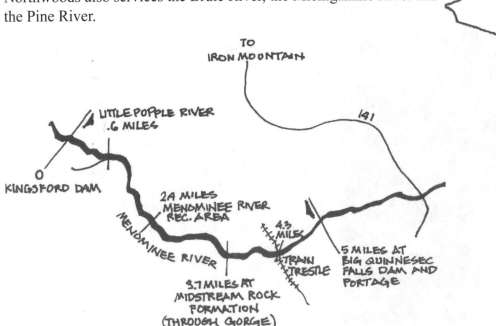

SOUNDTRACK: Six String Music – Jimmy Buffett, Whiskey Dreams – Iron Mountain Band, Dog Days Are Over – Florence & the Machine, Island Girl – Elton John, Guantanamera – the Sandpipers

RIVER QUOTES...
- Mister P: "It's a mini-Mississippi River"
- Randy (handing a life vest to Mister P): "This is the one you wore on the Brule last year, so it's been tested for floatation"

MILES: 486 NW of Detroit, 429 mi NW of Grand Rapids, 198 mi West of Mackinaw City, 117 mi SW of Christmas, 216 mi North of Milwaukee.

THE BACKGROUND: MENOMINEE RIVER

A few minutes northwest of Iron Mountain is where the confluence of the Michigamme and the Brule Rivers forms the origin of the Menominee River. Flowing southeast until it empties into the northwest edge of Lake Michigan at Green Bay (the body of water, not where the Packers play), all 115 miles of the Menominee River form the border between Wisconsin and the Upper Peninsula.

The Menominee is known as "the river of mist" for the mist that rises at the churning class 3 and 4 rapids of Piers Gorge, the wildest section of the 115 mile-long river (and downstream from this chapter's trip).

The section of the Menominee detailed in this chapter is in its upper reaches. We begin 2 miles downstream from the Menominee and Pine Rivers merger, at the Kingsford Dam. The dam was built in 1924 by Henry Ford to power his nearby manufacturing plant in Kingsford MI. After paddling 5 miles from the Kingsford Dam, the trip ends at the Big Quinnesec Falls Dam, built in 1912. This is a hard working river, with 12 hydroelectric-producing dams operating on it.

This 5-mile stretch of the Menominee is very beginner friendly. It's slow, quiet (at least on a weekday) and wide for the first half of the ride. The last half of the paddle provides you with some fabulous rock formations both midstream (unusual placements, and spectacular ones) and on the river banks.

From the Northwoods Wilderness Outfitters livery, Uncle Buck often serves as both driver to the launch site and local tour guide. You may want to ask for him, although it's possible that we caught him on a good day. As a friend of livery co-owner Randy noted, "You'll have a fine drive with Uncle Buck. Since he started taking his medication, he hardly ever blacks out while driving".

The heart of the Menominee Tribal cultural was where the river meets Green Bay. The name "Menominee" means "wild rice". These Native Americans paddled the local rivers in the pursuit of this staple of their diet.

Within the river's watershed, and definitely worth a viewing side trip, is the Menominee River tributary of Paint River and the Paint's exhilarating *"Horse Race Rapids"*. Locals refer to this wild whitewater stretch as "our little Grand Canyon". These rapids are a paddling adventure for only the most experienced – or perhaps the most crazy - kayakers. The rest of us should just walk alongside it for the spectacular view. The rapids rampage into a gorge where the river is swirling wildly, making a magnificent thundering sound as the rapids crash and slam their way over boulders through the steep-walled canyon. This is a great memory in the making for everyone who visits.

Horse Race Rapids directions: travel 14 miles NW of Florence WI (30 min. northwest of Iron Mountain) on US2 to Airport Road, turn right (east) on Airport until it ends at Paint River. You walk down a quarter-mile worth of steps to the rapids.

The Menominee River is considered an excellent stream for smallmouth bass fishing.

The crack researchers paddling the Menominee in mid-June were Mister P Pienta, Maggie and Doc.

THE RIVER:
PADDLING THE MENOMINEE

Launch 100 yards downstream from the Kingsford Dam. At the park access site are vault toilets, a shelter, picnic tables, grills and horseshoe pits. As you launch, the current is the swiftest it will be at any time over the 5 mile paddle. With few exceptions, this trip is down a river 20' to 25' deep and 150' to 200' wide.

.4 mi/8 min: on the left is an 80' tall viewing platform overlooking spectacular stands of pine and birch.

.6 mi/13 min: Little Popple River, a category two trout stream, merges from the right.

1.2 mi/24 min: on the mid-June float, Northern Star flowers are in full bloom along the left shore; the first of several homes are visible on your right. A curse and a blessing: the wide river provides no relief from strong headwinds kicked up (potentially giving you some pretty good exercise), but also keeps the black flies away (an occasional Menominee River problem).

1.4 mi/32 min: left of midstream you pass by a 120' long island just before paddling below the power lines.

1.7 mi/40 min: paddle by back-to-back small islands then a larger one. Big homes appear on the left, a farm on the right.

We're out here on a weekday when most pontoons & motorized fishing boats are docked, making it a good time to paddle. The depth of the Menominee River is very friendly to these craft.

2.2 mi/52 min: near the stone seawall on the left are a viewing platform, a dock, and homes.

2.4 mi/57 min: on the left is a boat landing of the Menominee River Recreation Area. There is a picnic area beyond the landing. The frequent riverside homes you now see belong to two towns, Kingsford, Michigan on the left and Aurora, Wisconsin on the right, causing Maggie to ask, "Do we need our passports to get out on the right shore?"

2.9 mi/1 hr 10 min: paddle below the Highway 95 Bridge where a brief run of shallow water reveals a rocky river-bottom beneath and beyond the bridge.

3.2 mi/1 hr 15 min: a boat launch sits on the right bank.

3.7 mi/1 hr 28 min: *a stunning site!* Sitting midstream is a beautifully-sculptured rock formation, formed by three separate, 30' tall rock islands. On the approach to these islands, the river narrows to 50' wide.

4 mi/1 hr 32 min: reach the tip of a large island. The wider passage is left, the right is fairly obstructed. Begin to paddle into a rock-walled gorge where you may encounter class 1 rapids, non-existent in the water levels during the trip taken for this book.

4.3 mi/1 hr 40 min: pass beneath the historic railroad bridge, built in 1895. Impressive rock walls as high as 70' chaperone you along both banks.

4.6 mi/1 hr 46 min: paddle out of the gorge and into a very wide lake, the backwater of the Big Quinnesec Falls Dam, visible ahead. "Quinnesec" is a Chippewa word referring to the smoke-like mist from the falls that rose high into the sky before the dam was built.

Stay on the left side of the lake on your approach to the take-out.

5 miles/1 hour 56 minutes: you're in! Take out at the dock on the left, just beyond the tip of a peninsula. There is a vault toilet at this access.

THE TOWN:
IRON MOUNTAIN

Detroit Tigers local radio affiliate: WMIQ 1450AM

Entering Iron Mountain on US2 from the west, you're greeted by a sign which reads, "Welcome to Iron Mountain, Proud Hometown of Tom Izzo and Steve Mariucci". The two met as local grade school rivals on the basketball court, before becoming teammates and best friends at the only high school in Iron Mountain. Attending Northern Michigan University together, Izzo became an All-American guard in basketball and Mariucci an All-American quarterback for the football team. Among the ways that the two men gave back to the community was by raising money for the state-of-the-art "Izzo-Mariucci Fitness Center", a wing built on to their old high school.

As a side note, in 1975 Northern Michigan U had the greatest one year improvement in NCAA football history, going from 0-10 in 1974 to 13-1 and the national championship in 1975, with Steve Mariucci at quarterback. Go Wildcats!

Iron Mountain is home to the *Pine Mountain Ski*

Jump. Built in the 1930s, this is the largest artificial ski jump in the world at 176' high and 380' long. Try walking up the wooden stairs right in the middle of the jump, as they become steeper and steeper. It creates an interesting sensation inside you. Or don't climb the ski jump: just standing at the base of the jump and looking out, the hilltop provides you with an incredible view to the northwest that includes 7 lakes and seems to stretch for miles. Another great visual is from the end of the observation deck that hangs well out over a sheer bluff (here comes that funny sensation again).

The Continental Cup Ski Jumping Competition is held on the Pine Mountain Ski Jump each year in mid-February. This is the #1 ski jump tournament in the USA for attracting top international skiers (as Pine Mountain is known world-wide as one of the top jumping hills anywhere).

Fred Pabst, of the Pabst Blue Ribbon Beer Family, founded the Pine Mountain Winter Recreation Area in the 1930s. What began with one gas-powered rope tow and a small warming shelter has grown into an area that entertains folks from around the world. Pabst – once again bringing joy to us all, God bless 'em.

"All gave some, and some gave all". On top of Pine Mountain, steps away from the ski jump, is the U. P. Veterans Memorial. The Memorial pays tribute to members of the armed forces and their memories. A 20' x 30' flag flies over the Memorial for all but 4 days of the year: during Memorial Day, Flag Day, the 4th of July, and Veterans Day, a 30' x 60' flag is flown.

The Upper Peninsula Sports Hall of Fame is located at Famer's Bar in the Pine Mountain Resort, adjacent to the ski jump (perfect: the U.P. Sports H.O.F. in a bar. *Sip one for the Gipper*). This is worth a visit for sports fans, with great memorabilia that dates back to the 1930s. Check it out at http://upshf.com/

Area camping: River Bends Campground has 160 sites on the banks of the Menominee River. River Bends has a swimming beach, playground, picnic area, boat access, and rents canoes and paddleboats. The campground is located at N3905 Pine Mountain Road in Iron Mountain, phone (906) 779-1171. River Bends is owned by Willie Erickson, 1959 U.S. National Ski Jumping Champion & a member of the 1960 USA Olympic team.

A few feet from renting your canoes & kayaks, Northwoods Wilderness Outfitters has a 2-bedroom cabin that sleeps 6. Call Randy or Cindy at (906) 774-9009 for reservations.

One of our favorite places for an overnight stay is in nearby Florence, WI at the Lakeside Bed and Breakfast. Lakeside B&B is a 12-minute drive from the Northwoods Wilderness Outfitters livery in Iron Mountain. The view from the second floor rooms overlooking scenic Fisher Lake is gorgeous. Each room has its own fireplace. Breakfast is served by candlelight and, more importantly, is as delicious as the dessert it's served with. Call Rita at (715) 528-3259. Lakeside is located on US2 10 miles west of the Northwoods livery.

For more area info, go to http://www.cityofironmountain.com/

THE TAVERN: GREENLEAF'S BAR

We liked Greenleaf's so much that during our 24-hour stay we visited twice. Greenleaf's Bar is also known as Flip's Greenleaf Bar & Grill. Outside, the pub had a wonderful, classic, throwback feel about it that initially drew us in. Inside, our excellent waitress (who happens to also be the owner), Lyn Flaminio, told us… the… rest… of the story…

The Greenleaf Family had the building constructed in 1953 (original owners still live next door). The building's entire space, now containing only the bar, was first built to house 3 businesses: the bar, a barber shop, and a confectionary. The beautiful old piano in the room on the right looks like it might have been played to celebrate that 1953 opening.

Pennants hang from the ceiling for the NMU Wildcats, the Michigan Tech Huskies, the Ferris State Bulldogs, and the MSU Spartans. As expected in the hometown of Tom Izzo, Greenleaf's feels like a Michigan State University campus pub: in addition to the various Green & White paraphernalia, there is a framed photo on the wall with an inscription, "To Rob and the Staff, Greenleaf Bar & Grill is still one of the best. Thank you for your support. Go State!" signed Tom Izzo. I was right at home in my "Go Green Go White Go Canoeing" t-shirt (although as an Eastern Michigan University grad, my green & white can go both ways. Not that there's anything wrong with that).

Within the bar is a small, intimate room with two pool tables. It's very comfortable with excellent lighting, enticing you to stay all day. The bar also offers video and dart games, big screen TVs, and live music each weekend. Outdoors, the back deck has 7 tables and a fine atmosphere for eating, drinking, and relaxing.

And then there was the food…

The burgers were char-grilled, good 'n juicy. Everyone raved about the breadsticks, "the best ever!" A little Ma & Pa place in town makes the homemade pizza for Greenleaf's – thin, tasty, and receiving a unanimous "mm mm good!" from crack researchers Maggie, Toni, Mister P, and Doc. Offered on the first Greenleaf's menu in 1953, still on the menu today, and getting two thumbs up is "Leon's homemade chicken dumpling soup". Mighty fine.

Greenleaf's Tavern is located at 1340 S. Carpenter Avenue at Detroit Avenue in Iron Mountain MI 49801, a few feet north of the town of Kingsford. Phone (906) 779-5000. Check out their website at www.flipsbar.com

Sources: Pine Mountain Ski Jump historical markers, Florence Wild Rivers Interpretive Center, National Park Service, Uncle Buck, Randy Gustafson, The Mining Journal, Lyn Flaminio

Lower Peninsula Rivers

AuSable

Black

Boardman

Cedar

Clinton

Crockery Creek

Flint

Grand

Manistee

Paw Paw

Pentwater North

Pigeon

Prairie

Red Cedar

Rouge/Detroit

St. Joseph

Shiawassee

AUSABLE RIVER
Mio MI
Trip 7.3 miles
1 hour & 47 minutes

Beginner Ability

Livery: Hinchman Acres Canoe Rental, 702 N. Morenci (M33), Mio MI 48647, (989) 826-3267, www.hinchman.com. Hinchman's is 4 blocks north of the M33 and M72 traffic light. Owners Natalie and Sam Giardina.

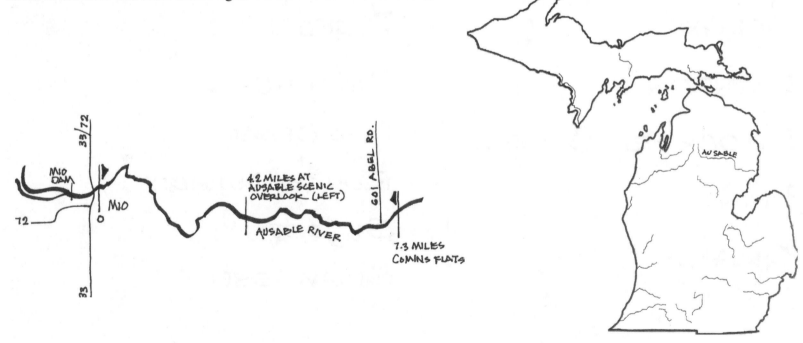

SOUNDTRACK: Joyce Country Ceili Band – Saw Doctors, In Spite of Ourselves – John Prine & Iris DeMent, Pipeline – George Bedard, Alive and Well and Living In – Jethro Tull, Dudley Do-Right

RIVER QUOTES...

- Kenny, commenting on a riverside boulder and Chris' penchant for collecting large river objects: "The unusual thing is that Chris' canoe is underneath the rock"
- Sign on the livery wall: "My wife says if I go fishing one more time, she will leave me. I'm gonna miss that woman"

MILES: 190 mi North of Detroit, 190 mi NE of Grand Rapids, 108 mi SE of Mackinaw City, 244 mi SE of Christmas, 456 mi NE of Milwaukee

THE BACKGROUND: AUSABLE RIVER

The AuSable River is arguably the best known and most popular river in all of Michigan. Paddlers love it, creating enough demand for rental canoes and kayaks that a dozen liveries operate along the river banks. Fishermen know the river as fertile ground for catching trout (considered one of the finest trout streams in the country), smallmouth bass, walleye, salmon and steelhead. Just east of

Grayling is the 8 miles of the river from Burton's Landing to Wakely Bridge known as the AuSable's "Holy Waters", the "no-kill, flies-only" stretch where all trout caught must be released.

The AuSable River begins flowing in the north central Lower Peninsula. Its headwaters form 70 miles south of the Mackinac Bridge where two creeks, the Bradford and the Kolka, merge near the town of Frederic (Frederic is 10 miles northwest of Grayling).

The river runs east for 130 miles, most of it from Grayling in the west to Oscoda in the east. It is in Oscoda where the AuSable ride ends as it empties into Lake Huron.

From Frederic through Grayling, the AuSable is a pretty little stream. Just beyond the Wakeley Bridge at the

M33, and ends a little over 7 miles downstream at Comins Flats. This beginner friendly 2-hour trip travels the very wide and 3' deep AuSable with no tricky or tight turns in a pleasantly-moving current absent of difficult obstructions.

The times posted in this chapter will be on the fast side as we ran the AuSable during early-Spring high water in mid-April.

On the 2 hours between today's launch and take-out, you won't be shortchanged on toilets and campsites: you'll paddle by one rest stop, 3 campgrounds, and one scenic overlook. Every one of them, except for the scenic overlook, has restrooms.

The wildlife viewing on the river was outstanding. Our crack researchers reported wood ducks, merganser ducks, blue herons, eagles and pileated woodpeckers on our journey.

Since 1947, the AuSable is home to the AuSable River Canoe Marathon. Held each year in July, the Marathon is a 120-mile long non-stop canoe race. It is the country's premier long distance canoe race, referred to as the world's toughest spectator sport. In a 1973 Sports Illustrated article on the race by author and Michigan native Jim Harrison, the 1972 champs memorably described their efforts as a "machine with two pistons". At 9PM in Grayling, it begins with a wild foot race of participants carrying their canoes towards the river. At full sprint, they arrive at the water's edge, launching into the river. Close to 50,000 spectators follow the race from bridges and

end of the Holy Waters, the river fattens from the additional volume of the merging South Branch and then the North Branch. About 13 miles downstream from the North Branch, 50 miles from its Frederic area headwaters, the AuSable arrives in Mio.

This is a hard working river, with Consumer's Energy generating power through a series of dams that they operate on the water. The first AuSable dam is the one at Mio, on the west side of M33. Beyond the dam the river widens but its speed does not slow.

The trip outlined in this chapter begins a few hundred feet downstream from the Mio Dam, to the immediate east of dams along the course. Paddling through the night in the total darkness of the Huron National Forest, the winner's arrive 15 hours later (close to noon the next day) at the finish line on the edge of Lake Huron in Oscoda. Expending up to 60 paddle strokes a minute, no one will confuse this athletic event with recreational paddling!

The crack researchers on the AuSable in mid-April were Jeff Cripe, Nadia Holyk, Vicki Schroeder, JJ Johnson, Ron Swiecki, Chris Weaks, Kenny Umphrey and Doc.

THE RIVER: PADDLING THE AUSABLE

Launch at the Mio M33 River Access, to the east and in sight of M33, on the AuSable's south bank. On this stretch of the water, the riverbed averages 150' wide and 3' deep (although there are isolated 6' deep holes).

.2 mi/4 min: the sign on the left bank reads, "Entering quality fishing area".

.8 mi/12 min: large rock, 6' diameter and 3' above the water line, near the left bank.

1.5 mi/21 min: *Loud's Rest Stop* is on the left bank, a break spot with restrooms and an access point for paddlers and anglers.

2 mi/27 min: you'll know that you're exactly two miles into the trip as you pass by a small brown house, fronted by a tiny dock, on the left shore. Adding more fun to the trip are the tree swallows, so many in number that they darken the sky, flying all around us.

2.8 mi/38 min: on the left shore are 20 steps leading up from the river to a 12' tall bluff. At the top of the bluff, a gap in the wood fence leads to the *AuSable Loop Campground*. There are vault toilets and drinking water here.

2.9 mi/39 min: a left bank sign reads, *River Dune / Huron-Manistee National Forest*, a hike-in campground with vault toilets. The view from the river is of a beautiful two-tiered wood wall with 14 steps leading up from the river.

3.7 mi/52 min: reach the upstream tip of the first of 3 back-to-back-to-back islands; on the left are stairs taking you from the AuSable to the top of a 30' tall bluff.

4.2 mi/1 hour: a sign for the *AuSable River Scenic Overlook* is on your left, with 60 steps taking you up to a height of 35'. Downstream from the Overlook takes you through a bouncy ride on light rapids.

5 mi/1 hr 10 min: on the right, a tiny creek merges followed by a gorgeous stand of pines running for 200' along the river.

5.2 mi/1 hr 13 min: *Meadow Springs* reads the sign on the left bank, a hike-in campsite with vault toilets. 12 steps take you from the river to the site.

5.7 mi/1 hr 22 min: at the end of a long straightaway, as the river bends right, is a 40' tall bluff with a wooden fence at its crest. This bluff runs for several hundred feet.

6.4 mi/1 hr 30 min: a series of homes appear on the right slope near a merging creek.

7.3 miles/1 hour 47 minutes: you're in! *Comins Flats* is the river access boat ramp on your left, complete with restrooms.

THE TOWN: MIO

Detroit Tigers local radio affiliate: WAVC 93.9FM

Mio is located at the junction of M33 and M72, between Grayling and Oscoda, on the southern banks of the AuSable. Founded in 1881 by two men, Henry Deyarmond and Coolige Comins, the town was named in honor of Henry's wife, Mioe, with its name shortened to Mio in 1883. The river's *Comins Flats* access in turn was named after Coolige Comins.

Mio is home to a couple of special and rare wildlife species: the Thunderbolts, the name of their school sports teams, and the Kirtland Warbler. The Warbler is an endangered bird, with only an estimated 4,000 in existence. It is not only paddlers and fishermen that flock to the area, but also bird watchers drawn from all over the world for a look at this rare bird. Kirtland Warblers nest almost exclusively within a 50 mile radius of Mio, and winter 1,250 miles south in the Bahama Islands.

Why Mio? Except for a very few spots in the U.P., Mio is the only place in the world with the needed mix of young jack pine trees, sandy soils, and small grass openings that the bird needs to breed successfully. Since Warblers build their nests on the ground, to protect their eggs and babies the DNR closes their breeding areas to the public during breeding season.

Ironically, improved forest fire prevention techniques have worked against the bird, reducing their breeding space: the Warblers require young jack pine trees no taller than 20'. Without wildfires, the forests grow too old and too tall for the Kirtland Warbler to nest in. Controlled burns, intentionally started fires by the U.S. Forest Service, are prescribed to help continue the species.

Maps for a 58-mile, self-guided, *Jack Pine Wildlife Viewing Tour,* including the home grounds of the Kirtland Warbler, are available at the US Forest Service, Mio Ranger Office, on the east side of M33 just north of town, (989) 826-3252.

Mio is home to the *Noreast'r Music & Art Festival,* held annually at the Oscoda County Fairgrounds. Appearing are a great variety of bands from all over the country, including many from Michigan (like Ann Arbor's Dick Siegel and the Brandos: "eggs over easy, hash browns 'n you, we'll go to Angelo's"). Since 2004, the organizers have kicked up the cool by giving away 12 guitars each year at the festival. These are for kids under 18 who have a sincere interest in music, a great way to encourage the next generation. Check out the festival website at www.noreastr.net.

Canoeing and kayaking, trout fishing, bird watching, wildlife viewing, great hiking, ORV and snowmobile trails all make Mio a wonderful destination for the sportsman or woman. Downtown has several sporting goods stores and bait & tackle shops to meet their needs. The storefront sign in the window at *Clancy's Bargain Barn* was the one that really caught our attention, *"Open most days about 10 or 11, occasionally as early as 9:00, but some days as late as 12 or 1, we close about 4 or 5 but sometimes as late as 6 or 7. Some days we arn't here at all, and lately I've been here just about all the time, except when I'm someplace else"*, signed Clancy.

Area camping: there are 3 sites along the river on the M33 to Comins Flats trip:

The *AuSable Loop* is the only one of the 3 riverside campgrounds that you can drive in to. As with the other two, you can also paddle up to it. From the site's scenic overlook, you get a great, elevated, panoramic view of the AuSable River. No reservations are required for the Loop's 5 sites. The campground includes vault toilets and drinking water. There

are no electric or water hookups. From Mio, take M33 one-half mile north to McKinley Road, turn right and go 3 miles to the campground sign, turn right towards the river.

The *River Dune Campground* is a hike-in and paddle up campsite. The site has vault toilets, no drinking water. There is a one-half mile hike in to the campground from the parking lot at the AuSable Loop campground.

The *Meadow Springs Campground* is a hike-in and paddle up site, used primarily by canoers and kayakers. The site has vault toilets, no drinking water. It is located on the edge of a beautiful red pine forest. Take M33 north from Mio for 1/2 mile to McKinley Road and turn right. Travel 3 miles, turn right at the entrance and follow the signs.

A fine option to camping is to stay in one of the lodges at the canoe and kayak livery, Hinchman Acres. The lodges sit along two fishing lakes, and are very comfortable & clean. Some of the lodges come with a fireplace. Hinchman's lodges make for a great post-paddling retreat, and Natalie and her dog Max are wonderfully pleasant hosts. If you visit Hinchman early or late in the season, you may see Max wearing one of his jaunty red sweaters.

THE TAVERN: MA DEETER'S

Ma Deeter's has your attention even before you walk inside. Their parking lot sign says, "This is God's County. Please Don't Drive Thru Town Like Hell". You know how it is when you walk into a tavern for the first time, and immediately you realize that you'll be coming back again? That's Ma Deeter's.

You step inside Ma's front door and you walk into 1941. According to Ma's manager Brian Michael…

* The building's basement was poured in 1940 and the doors opened in 1941. Originally this log cabin bar and boarding house (rooms upstairs) also served as the town's post office and general store.
* There are two original 1941 sets of tables and chairs still in use (our honor to be at one).
* The original tavern fireplace keeps on hummin' (with the help of an insert box) when continuously fed wood by the staff on chilly days and nights.
* A former Ma's owner was the brother of Jack Stefani, a member of Detroit's infamous Purple Gang (Prohibition-era, particularly rough, gangsters)
* Ma's holds the only surviving "Gold" liquor license in Michigan, i.e. you can buy a fifth of liquor to go (once you don't renew the license, you lose it). You have to be operating a looooong time to have one of these…

Anna (Ma) Deeter and her husband William arrived in Luzerne in 1903. The original Ma Deeter's was a different building than today's Ma's. It opened in 1921, was located one block north of town, and for 20 years provided a large number of hunters and fishermen with food and a place to sleep.

The Ma Deeter's that you see today has beautiful interior pine construction including four thick wooden supports spread out across the bar room floor. Rows of hooks suspended from the ceiling are for snowmobile and motorcycle helmets and, Kenny suggested, unruly customers.

Sunshine and Ray Marlin Tweedly purchased Ma's in 1988, wisely leaving the pub's name the same. Inserted into a tavern wall is a light box memorial to the late Ray, R.I.P. 2.18.10. The outdoor section of Ma's is "Sunshine's Garden", a tribute to Ray's wife. There is dance space in both Sunshine's Garden and indoors for line dancing and other types of moving to the occasional live entertainment.

The food at Ma's is excellent! Chris said that there was no chewing required on the ribs. For the very tasty all-you-can-eat walleye, Kenny asked waitress Patty if there was a time limit, thinking he'd pick up tomorrow where he left off today (turns out there is). One person after another came through Ma's front door for carryout pizza, in a stream so steady that it looked like a conga line. When we asked customers for their opinion of the pizza's taste, they spoke in reverent and hushed tones. A bar sign read, "Ma Deeter's homemade pork rinds. When pigs fly, maybe they'll be able to escape. Until then, we'll keep making our pork rinds".

In each chapter's "The Tavern" section, you're directed to a bar that is usually nearby the river, but Ma's is in the town of Luzerne, 7 miles west of Mio and this chapter's AuSable trip. I made an exception for Ma's on the advice of Big Al VanKerckhove, a friend and member of the "Friends of the Rouge", a paddling and environmental group. It was sage advice, as it turned out. Thank you Al!

And of course, Ma Deeter's serves Pabst Blue Ribbon Beer, always a sure sign of quality.

Ma Deeter's is located at 2262 Deeter Road, M72 & County Road 490, in Luzerne MI 48636. Phone (989) 826-1013. Check out their website at www.madeeterslodge.com

Sources: Natalie Giardina, flyanglersonline.com, Mio historical markers, www.n-sport.com, DNR, U.S. Forest Service, Info MI, Al VanKerckhove, Brian Michael

BLACK RIVER
South Haven MI
Trip 6.3 miles
2 hours & 18 minutes

Intermediate Ability

Livery: Kayak Kayak, 360 Douglas Avenue, Holland MI 49424; (616) 366-1146,www.kayak-kayak.com. Owner Skip Nagelvoort. Kayak-Kayak also services the Grand and the Kalamazoo rivers.

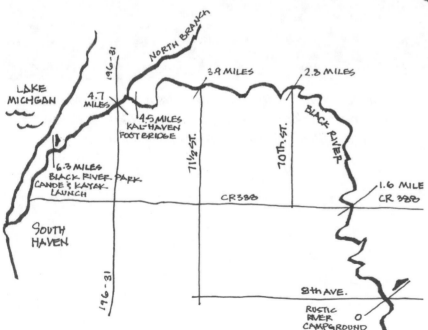

SOUNDTRACK: Hey Ho – Gin Wigmore, Express Yourself – Watts 103rd St Rhythm Band, Takin' Care of Business - BTO, Bring Me Sunshine – the Jive Aces, I'm Going Back to Old South Haven – Orley Johnston

RIVER QUOTE...

Maggie: "I'm using natural sun block - the trees"

MILES: 180 mi West of Detroit, 57 mi SW of Grand Rapids, 293 mi SW of Mackinaw City, 421 mi South of Christmas, 213 mi SE of Milwaukee

THE BACKGROUND: BLACK RIVER

The 6 mile section of the Black River outlined in this chapter is part of the river's South Branch. This section is within the final 21 miles of the South Branch that runs in a generally northwesterly direction from Bangor in the east to South Haven in the west. It is in South Haven that the river empties into Lake Michigan. These 21 miles are referred to as the *Bangor / South Haven Heritage Water Trail*.

The Bangor/ South Haven Heritage Water Trail Association is a volunteer group that is working to develop the 21 miles into a place that readily comes to mind when paddlers are looking for a fun river getaway. They work to keep the river clean, to cut a path for canoers and kayakers through logjams, and to develop riverside signs that educate folks who are using the Black about its local history and the environment. You can check on the association's progress and river updates at www.vbco.org/watertrail.asp.

The Two Rivers Coalition is a citizen based group working to advocate, conserve and educate folks about the Black River and the Paw Paw River watersheds. Learn more at www.tworiverscoalition.org.

The suggested 6 mile trip is like two completely different, and very cool, adventures…

- In part one, the river is secluded with a bayou feel to it. You paddle beneath a shaded canopy of trees (thus Maggie's river quote) on a narrow, shallow and windy river full of deadwood paddling challenges.
- In part two, the canopy disappears and the narrow stream widens and deepens. Long straight-aways replace the constant twisting and turning. You're paddling by houseboats and fine looking riverside homes, and through a marina among big boats, with owners socializing and greeting you as they sip in their slips while you kayak or canoe by. Lake Michigan looms ahead.

The assigned degree of difficulty rating of "Intermediate" is due to the continuous maneuvering required around plentiful river deadwood in the first part of the trip (this will be minimized due to the on-going efforts of the Bangor/ South Haven Heritage Water Trail Association) and the occasional waves created by those big boats in the second part of the trip.

The Black includes a healthy population of trout and salmon for the fishing minded.

The crack research team on the Black in late-July was Mister P Pienta, Maggie and Doc.

THE RIVER: PADDLING THE BLACK

Launch on the east side of South Haven at the 8th Avenue "Rustic River Campground" (campground details may be found at the end of this chapter's "The Town" section) just west of 68th Street. As you begin paddling, the river is 35' wide and 3' deep.

.8 mi/11 min: encounter the first of 3 fallen trees spanning the entire river within the first river mile. No portages are required. A creek merges to the right as the river bends left.

1 mi/21 min: from the left, a small crick merges; crack researcher Mister P tells us that "there's a creek, a crick, and a dribble… and this is a crick".

3 minutes downstream, a 12' wide creek (not a crick) merges on your left. 5' down the creek is a collapsed footbridge.

You're paddling through the Dragonfly Kingdom, God bless 'em all, which is why mosquitoes are a minimal problem.
1.5 mi/30 min: a pipe 2' in diameter extends out over the river's edge, discharging water into the Black River. 3 of these pipes will be seen on this section of the river.

1.6 mi/35 min: paddle beneath County Road 388, also known as Phoenix Road (the street that is, to the west, downtown South Haven's main thoroughfare).

2.2 mi/46 min: the very clogged Butternut Creek merges from the right at a left bend in the river; the creek precedes the first sandy bluff viewed today, 20' tall on the left.

2.4 mi/49 min: a fallen tree is completely across the river, allowing a 3' clearance to paddle below; 1 minute beyond is a short island midstream that is passable left or right.
2 minutes later, a tiny creek merges right, long and straight.

2.8 mi/57 min: just after a small creek empties into the Black, you paddle below the 70th Street Bridge. Until now, the river had been flowing north. It will now turn to the west, pointed towards Lake Michigan, with the **Kal-Haven Trail** (a multi-use trail linking South Haven to Kalamazoo) running alongside on the river's right (north).

1 minute past the bridge and on the left is a 50' long sandy beach, one of the first good break spots today.

3.1 mi/1 hour: the first home seen today is a very nice one, sitting on a 30' tall bluff on the right, with a screened-in deck. The river reaches its widest yet today at 50'.

3.3 mi/1 hr 7 min: a large creek, 25' wide at its mouth, enters on the left. Downstream 5 minutes, another creek merges left. Maggie notes that the bugs are dancing on the river's surface for us, the sun gleaming off of them, like little crystals on top of the water.

3.9 mi/1 hr 22 min: arrive at the 71 ½ Street Bridge. This marks the point where your shaded canopy is no more (we are drenched in sunshine). Fishermen throwing lines in from the river bank are catching catfish.

4.4 mi/1 hr 35 min: at the end of a long straight-away, the river bends right at the base of a high bluff; the home at the top of the bluff faces upstream with a fabulous river view.

4.5 mi/1 hr 40 min: looking like a park is private property on your left. Just beyond is the beautiful covered bridge of the Kal-Haven

Trail. The Kal-Haven will now be running along the left (the south) side of the river the balance of your trip.

Visible downstream from the covered bridge is the North Branch of the Black River, merging from your right. The river widens and is now one kayak paddle length deep. At this merger, paddle to your left to stay on the river's South Branch.

4.7 mi/1 hr 43 min: paddle beneath the bridges of the 196/31 north & southbound lanes.
Homes are seen beyond the right bank. Pontoon boats appear on the water.

5 miles/1 hr 50 min: pass below the Blue Star Memorial

Highway/A2. Just beyond and docked along the left shore are houseboats and Cary Grant and Sophia Loren flashbacks.

There are nice looking homes as you paddle into the marina area past motor yachts lined up in their slips. It's fun to banter with the boat owners and check out the names they've picked out for their babies. "Tipsy Smile" and "A Tad Too Much"… we're beginning to develop a theme here.

5.9 mi/2 hrs 10 min: the "Marine Travel Lift" is on your left.

6.3 miles/2 hours 18 minutes: you're in! On the left, just past the small dock, is a gently sloping dirt landing at which to exit the river. You've arrived at the Black River Park Canoe & Kayak Launch, a part of the Black River Park Marina. The Canoe & Kayak Launch is located a few feet north of the nexus of the universe at the intersection of Dunkley and Dunkley.

From here, Lake Michigan is one river mile away, always an option to paddle to.

THE TOWN: SOUTH HAVEN

Detroit Tigers local radio affiliate: WCSY 103.7 FM

South Haven is a beautiful little Lake Michigan shoreline town in the southwest corner of Michigan. Along the Big Lake you'll find seven public beaches (each groomed daily) and multiple boat access points for Lake Michigan, all within the city limits. Lake Michigan sunsets in South Haven have enchanted well before settlers arrived from Europe.

In the late-1700s, Native Americans named the land "Ni-Ko-Nong" or "beautiful sunsets".

South Haven lies within Van Buren County, the "Blueberry Capital of the World" (#1 in the USA in blueberry production), the state's leader in grape production, and the home of more fruit acreage than any other Michigan county. Within South Haven's borders are 12 farm markets and U-pick locations.

The town has been a major summer resort getaway since the early-1900s, drawing folks from the largest cities in the Midwest and beyond. With the 1911 opening of the West Michigan Pike (today's US31/Blue Star Highway), visitors could now drive here, and the tourism boom was on.

The charming little downtown Phoenix Street and surrounding streets and alleyways are enticing even on a rainy day. There are plenty of fun and unique adventures of interest including the Farmer's Market, antique shops, boutiques, bakeries, and restaurants. If you need a little direction, the extremely enthusiastic and helpful folks at the Tourism Bureau on Main Street are there to help.

Black River Books is a great place to browse, the retirement dream of owners Dick and Pam Haferman. 330 Kalamazoo St, (269) 637-7374, www.blackriverbooks.net. Inside, I found a copy of *Laughing Whitefish* by Robert Traver (aka John Voelker), a book that I'd been hunting for quite some time. Strangely enough, every book at BRB is marked down from $100 (a humorous marketing ploy).

You WILL want to taste the ice cream at Sherman's, located just east of downtown at 1601 Phoenix Street. There was a reason that we counted 30 people entering Sherman's within a 2-minute time period. This ice cream is delicious! Sherman's lets you know why their ice cream is soooo good on their website www.shermanicecream.com.

4th of July weekend's *Summer Art Fair* has been held annually since 1958. The town's events calendar is jam-packed. Check it at www.southhavenmi.com.

A wonderful hiking trail has its west end trailhead on Wells Street in South Haven, the Kal-Haven Trail. This 33 & one-half mile trail runs east-west, linking South Haven to Kalamazoo. The Kal-Haven Trail was opened in 1991 and was built on the abandoned Kalamazoo & South Haven Railroad route, which was in use from 1870 to 1970. The old railroad bed was converted to a trail with a limestone/slag surface and makes an excellent hiking and biking trail, taking you through quaint villages, open farmland, wooded terrain and dense brush. When there is a snow base of at least 4", snowmobiling is allowed. Running parallel is a separate trail, the Kal-Haven Horse Trail. Where County Road 687 meets the Kal-Haven Trail, there are hitching posts and an area large enough to accommodate horse trailers.

The South Pierhead Lighthouse is open the 3rd weekend each June (during Harborfest) for free public tours. The original 37' tall wooden tower was constructed in 1872, replaced in 1903 by the current 35' tall steel structure which stands at the end of an iron catwalk.

South Haven has a rich nautical history and many stories and artifacts from that history are yours to experience at the Michigan Maritime Museum. On *Friends Good Will* you can stand on the bow as you sail out on to Lake Michigan on the working replica of an 1810 tall ship. The museum is north of downtown and a few feet west of the Black River Bridge on 260 Dyckman Avenue, (269) 637-8078, www.michiganmaritimemuseum.org.

Lodging is not a problem in South Haven on weekdays, but on weekends books ahead. Historic inns, B&Bs, family-owned resorts, motels & hotels, and vacation rentals are everywhere.

For more information on lodging or anything else to do with South Haven, check www.southhaven.org.

Camping is available at the launch site of today's trip, the Rustic River Campground. Their address is 68840 8th Avenue, South Haven 49090. Phone (269) 637-3064.

THE TAVERN: CURVE INN

On the south side of town, on Blue Star Highway south of M140, you'll happily find the Curve Inn. Since 2007, the tavern has been owned by sisters Pat Clausen and Susan Villwock. The sisters' ancestors, known by the last name of Fellows, were homesteading members of the original group of South Haven settlers when Michigan was becoming a state in the 1830s.

The outside of the bar greets you with fluttering Pabst Blue Ribbon beer pennants and a sign that reads "Wood Fired Pizza". Even before you reach the front door, you can smell the goodness within. Inside, signs everywhere read "Well butter my buns and call me a biscuit: PBR 10 oz for $1, 22 oz for $2". I'm getting that tingling feeling all over. Smack in the middle of the 7 beers featured on the tappers is Pabst. Oh, I do like this place.

The Curve Inn is a very comfortable small box of a tavern at about 40' x 40'. You feel as if you're in the basement bar of a great friend, a place you'll want to come back to often. This building has been a tavern since the 1930s. Back in the day this was a workingman's bar and there was an industrial park full of factories out the tavern's back door. So many factory folks made their way here between shifts that there was dirt path worn into the grass leading to the bar's backdoor (proving Jimmy Mong's 1975 assertion that grass grows by inches and dies by feet).

An adjacent courtyard, maybe bigger than the bar, holds 6 picnic tables. Tents provide shelter above each table. Great circular fire pit! The courtyard's piece de resistance is a wood-fired oven with 4" thick refractory fire brick rated at 4,000 degrees, originally part of a foundry furnace from the old nearby industrial area. The oven's door was built from a fireplace insert found in a local scrap yard. The pizza is cooked next to the wood at 600 degrees, giving you get the taste of real wood in each pizza. Pulled pork sandwiches are also roasted outside in the wood fired oven.

The burgers are pressed fresh every morning, never frozen. These are excellent and NO condiments are needed. All soups are homemade and served with a slice of Parmesan garlic toast. The menu proclaims "World's Best Cream of Mushroom Soup" and Maggie agrees that "it's the best I've ever had!" Like a Justin Verlander fastball that gets faster deeper into the game, the fries get better deeper into the basket. A lot of "mm, mm" and smiling and nodding at each other while we ate.

There's a traffic light sitting on the bar. If the green light is lit, you'll read "Bar is open"; if the yellow light is on it reads "Last Call"; the red light tells you "Bar is closed". Obey.

Curve Inn has two pool tables, video machines, Keno, big screen TVs, and an old time "grip test machine".

Among the musical acts regularly performing at the Curve Inn is Muddy Waters' daughter, blues singer Joyce Walker. Joyce brings hall-of-fame blues stars with her when she sings. *"I'm a dirty old woman with a dirty old mind tonight".* You tell 'em Joyce! Before you leave, make sure to sign the ceiling.

The Curve Inn is located at 10336 Blue Star Memorial Hwy (the old West Michigan Pike), South Haven, MI 49090. Their phone number is (269) 637-5070.

Sources: South Haven Tourism Bureau, Skip Nagelvoort, Friends of the Kal-Haven Trail, Pat Clausen

Boardman River

Traverse City, MI
Trip 11.3 miles/ 3 hours

Intermediate Ability

Livery: Lyf Motiv Adventures,
205 Garland Street, Traverse City MI 49684;
 (231) 944-1146, www.lyfmotifadvs.com.
Owner Eric Clone. LMA requires you to drive your own vehicle to the
take out point and you will be shuttled to the put-in.

WEST ARM
BOARDMAN
LAKE

EAST ARM
GRAND TRAVERSE
BAY

TRAVERSE CITY

M 57

LONG RIFFLES &
CLASS I RAPIDS

BEITNER
RD

II MILES

6.8 MILES
SHUMSKY ACCESS

1.2
MILES

BOARDMAN RIVER

O BROWN E

6.4
MILES

JAXON CRK.

SWAINSTON CRK.

EAST CRK.

BOARDMAN

RIVER QUOTE Tracie: "Someone's going to have to pee in the river to bring up the water level" (author's note: fortunately, that wasn't necessary)

SOUNDTRACK: Travelling riverside blues – Led Zeppelin, cast your fate to the wind – Vince Guaraldi, Beer Drinkin' Woman – Memphis Slim & Willie Dixon, I'm Just Here to Ride the Train – Mountain Heart, Take Me to the River – Talking Heads

MILES: 255 mi NW of Detroit, 140 mi North of Grand Rapids, 103 mi SW of Mackinaw City, 231 mi SE of Christmas, 408 mi NE of Milwaukee

THE BACKGROUND: BOARDMAN RIVER

The Boardman River comes to an end as it flows through the heart of downtown Traverse City, where it empties into the West Arm of Grand Traverse Bay. The journey of the river and its major tributaries begins 50 river miles to the east, a little northeast of Kalkaska, where the Boardman's North Branch rises up from the Mahan swamp. The North Branch winds southwest for 24 miles until it merges with the 10 mile long South Branch at Supply Road. This North and South branch confluence, known as "the Fork", forms the beginning of the 26 mile long Boardman River Main branch. Right in the middle of the 26 mile long Main branch is where this chapter's trip takes place.

This 11 mile run begins about 20 driving minutes southeast of downtown Traverse City, and just a few feet downstream, and within sight, of the Brown Bridge Dam. The take out is at Beitner Road, 1 & 1/2 miles east of M37. The current is a brisk 4 mph as the water level drops an average of 8' per mile. *This is a fun river run!* The Boardman riffles, great in number, whip you quickly around the river bends. There are frequent encounters with privately-owned footbridges spanning the river, varying in look and design from near-rickety to unique creations built from old rail cars. The often-viewed homes along the shoreline do not intrude on the Boardman's solitude. Occasional bottom-skimming rarely results in getting stuck on the river floor.

For the fishing folk, the Boardman is thick with brook and brown trout, and is considered to be one of the top ten trout streams in Michigan.

Maggie and I floated this wonderful waterway with the Traverse Area Paddle Club. The TAPC was formed in 1999 to plan canoeing & kayaking outings with a group of friends. They have since grown from a social paddling group only to an environmental / paddling group, organizing river cleanups that involve the larger community. The TAPC's good steward activities have gone beyond the Boardman to include cleanups on the Sturgeon, Platte, AuSable, Betsie, Jordan, and the Pine. We in Michigan are blessed to have TAPC members residing among us. Check out the website at www.traverseareapaddleclub.org.

Crack researchers paddling the Boardman on this gorgeous October day were TAPC members Lois Goldstein, John Heiam, Tracie Lord, Deena Barshney, Roseanne Bowman, Dawn Freels, Mary Lee Orr, Marlene Puska, Marv Puska, Fred Swartz and Jocelyn Trepte, along with Maggie and Doc.

THE RIVER:
PADDLING THE BOARDMAN

Launch southeast of Traverse City at the Brown Bridge Road access, on Brown Bridge Road and 1/4 mile east of Arbutus Hill Road. Paddling begins 200 yards downstream from the Brown Bridge Dam, located at the western edge of the Brown Bridge Pond. Within the stretch of the Boardman outlined in this chapter, the river depth varies from bottom-scraping to 2' and the width from 25' to 35'.

.3 mi/5 min: paddle through the Brown Bridge Road dual culverts. On the approach the river shallows from 2' to 6". Immediately beyond the bridge stay right of center to avoid bottoming out on the shallow river floor.

.4 mi/8 min: a little creek merges from the left. Garfield Road traffic is soon audible as several homes are visible along the right shore.

.7 mi/12 min: float below the Garfield Road Bridge. 1 minute downstream is a nice log cabin on the left bank. Merging left with the Boardman on the cabin's upstream boundary is the 3.5 mile long East Creek.

1 mi/17 min: at exactly 1 mile into the trip, the river bends right and a small creek snakes its way through the marsh on your right, working its way to a river merger.

1.2 mi/20 min: 5 miles long is the fast-moving Swainston Creek, merging from the left. Two minutes downstream, where the river bends left, stay right of center or risk running aground in the very shallow water.

1.4 mi/25 min: paddle beneath the power lines just before the river meanders right.

1.6 mi/28 min: the footbridge crossing the river is just before the white house along East River Drive on the right.

2 mi/34 min: where the river bends right you're alongside the railroad tracks sitting upon a 20' high bluff on the left. 2 minutes downstream and along the right bank is a private residence with an old dance hall sign next to it announcing "The Brook / Beer-Dance".

2.3 mi/39 min: you're below the East River Road Bridge. 1 minute downstream and on the right is a red cottage and its sign that tells you "Core since 1926". From this cottage, an

elevated line runs across the river on which is displayed a flag almost as wide as the Boardman itself.

2.6 mi/43 min: beyond the left shore home, pass beneath a tiny footbridge. A wonderful and long riffles run is, to quote Robin Trower, about to begin.

3 mi/49 min: the 3-mile mark is noted by a neat landmark on the left shore, a totem pole next to a home.

3.2 mi/52 min: on the left is a fine looking log and stone home with a beautiful stone chimney. The home is located at the end of a long straightaway just before the river takes a dogleg right. Around the bend and on a right bank hill are stairs christened by Maggie as "the stairs to nowhere".

3.4 mi/54 min: paddle under the 2nd East River Road Bridge followed a few feet later by a classic old wooden railroad trestle.

3.8 mi/1 hr: encounter the first of two footbridges separated by one river minute.

4 mi/1 hr 5 min: as you paddle below power lines, there's an excellent 4 mile landmark and a fine break spot just left of midstream: 3 consecutive islands.

4.5 mi/1 hr 14 min: a home on the left with a stone lower level precedes two footbridges spaced one minute apart.

5.1 mi/1 hr 25 min: the pedestrian bridge crossing the Boardman is followed by majestic birch trees at the end of a straightaway. 5 minutes downstream is another footbridge.

6 mi/1 hr 38 min: the footbridge sign reads, "Beitner Road Bridge – 1 hour and 1/2 downstream". Close by and on the left shore is a home with a stone chimney. In 7 minutes you'll be at the next footbridge.

6.4 mi/1 hr 46 min: the gorgeous creek merging from your left is the 5.5 mile long Jaxon Creek. Just around the next bend is yet another footbridge, this one with a black gate.

6.8 mi/1 hr 53 min: the footbridge sign announces the approaching "Shumsky Access" which is one minute downstream and on the right. The *Traverse Area Paddle Club* knows the Boardman very well, and says that the stretch from Shumsky to Beitner Road (where today's trip ends) can get very crowded on summer weekends.

7.6 mi/2 hrs 5 min: there's a pedestrian bridge just before the white house on the right shore. At the next left bend keep right to avoid the very shallow water running from midstream to the left bank.

7.8 mi/2 hrs 9 min: the Boardman swings to the right around a home sitting on a peninsula. A pretty waterfall cascades into the river from the left.

8 mi/2 hrs 12 min: the river bends left as you float beneath a footbridge through shallow water. Just past the bridge and on the left is a footpath marked by a "Hoyt House" sign.

8.6 mi/2 hrs 22 min: *l-o-o-n-g riffles run.* You're below a pedestrian bridge and paddling through a great section of the river, fast with a light churn to it.

9.2 mi/2 hrs 30 min: the river flows beneath a green pedestrian bridge created from an old railroad car.

9.9 mi/2 hrs 40 min: a creek flows through the opening in a wooden seawall along the right bank. Behind the seawall is a good looking brown home.

10 mi/2 hrs 43 min: to your right, traffic is visible 150' away on River Road. The footbridge ahead tells you you're at Wicksall Bridge.

10.2 mi/2 hrs 46 min: *great class one rapids* takes you past a red barn on the approach to a footbridge. Two minutes beyond, an island lies right of midstream. There's a very nice light rapids run to the left of the island.

10.9 mi/2 hrs 56 min: just after the river turns left, paddle below the 2nd pedestrian bridge seen today that is created from an old railroad car.

11 miles/3 hours: you're in! The dock at the Beitner Road Access is on your right - take out here. There is a restroom at the access. The dock is a few feet before the dual culverts where the Boardman flows beneath the Beitner Road Bridge.

THE TOWN: TRAVERSE CITY

Detroit Tigers local radio affiliate: WTCM 580 AM

In 1847, an adventurer named Captain Boardman purchased land where a river flowed north into a bay. A town grew up around the merger of these two bodies of water, a town that would, in 1852, become known as Traverse City. The name was given by French traders due to the "long crossing" (*la grand traverse*) required to canoe across the bay. By 1900, this young town had a population of 6,000 people, serviced by 14 churches, 21 saloons, and 3 bordellos.

In Traverse City, the turn of the last century was full of wild days and colorful characters. One such character was brewery owner Frank Kratochvil. When Frank arrived, you knew that the party had started. This was only partly because, as brewery owner, he was the one who turned the taps on. Frank had a gift for making the time spent at his imbibing emporium memorable for friends and customers. He would get the party started by dancing several songs while balancing a full beer on his head. It was said that Frank never spilled a drop. Another late-1800s/early-1900s character was big Duff MacDonald, bartender at the Hurry Back Saloon on Front Street. With his enormous stature and turned up mustache, Duff bore a striking resemblance to Germany's Kaiser Wilhelm. Strangely, Duff also was a dead ringer for the town's only millionaire at the time, Perry Hannah, a man old enough to be Duff's Dad.

64

Although Captain Boardman purchased the first tract of land in what would become Traverse City, it was Perry Hannah who is considered to be the town's founding father. Hannah and fellow Chicago businessman Tracy Lay were the driving forces in growing Traverse City from a remote settlement in 1847 to, by 1880, the dominant industrial, timber, and retail hub in Northern Michigan.

Perry Hannah first saw the area while taking a boat trip down Captain Boardman's namesake in 1851. Hannah was scouting for pine and he wasn't disappointed. Hannah, Lay & Co. owned 50,000 acres within a few years, and their sawmill cut 400 million board feet. Their company built the town's first retail store, operated the first schooners and passenger boats to Chicago, and organized the town's first bank. The Traverse City experience made millions for Perry Hannah, and he returned the favor many times over…

- donating large tracts of land to churches, schools, and the city,
- donating land and counsel to prospective business owners – even encouraging folks to open businesses that would compete against Hannah, Lay, & Co.,
- pioneered the idea of the town as a summer resort destination, and invested the time, money and effort to make it happen,
- opened the area to tourism and investment by influencing Michigan to build a state road from Newaygo (just north of Grand Rapids) to Northport (just north of Traverse City) in 1859,
- and furthered that tourism/business opening by making the first rail line into town a reality in 1872.

Perry Hannah passed away at his Traverse City Sixth Street mansion in 1904, a few days before he was to turn 80. Active until the end, in 1903 he set the granite cornerstone of the Traverse City State Bank. This building still stands today as the home of downtown's Fifth Third Bank.

The pine trees that first attracted Perry Hannah to the area were more plentiful than the gorgeous rivers in Michigan. Up until the mid-1800s, the pine forest stretched for miles, so thick that the waters of Grand Traverse Bay could not be seen until you were standing on its shore. In the narrow space between the trees, footpaths of the Chippewas and Ottawas (who settled here a little over 100 years before Captain Boardman) cut here and there through the immense woodland. The rare open space was filled with a rich bounty of wild raspberries and blackberries, and the ground carpeted with daisies.

Once the timber interests began their work in earnest in the 1850s, this rich forest and the lifestyles that the area's Native Americans knew were forever lost. Employees from the lumber camps in the area worked hard and, in the little time off that they had, played hard. Lumberjacks would descend on the business district, first for a shave and a haircut and maybe some new clothes, then on to the saloons – sometimes for days at a time. These boys could be considerate drunks. After one wild Halloween party night, every outhouse in town had been turned over, except the six that belonged to widow gals.

One fascinating piece of local history was centered a few minutes north of Traverse City, on the Old Mission Peninsula. In 1839, a Presbyterian missionary named Peter Dougherty established the area's first permanent settlement near the northern tip of the peninsula in the village of Old Mission. Here, Peter founded a small colony where Native Americans and non-Indians lived and worked side-by-side as artisans, farmers, and teachers. The community thrives to this day, although you can easily take yourself back in time to the 1830s by visiting the town's original structures, still standing and still in use, including the mission house, the general store and the church.

A drive through the beautiful and historic Old Mission Peninsula is time well spent. The peninsula is a thin finger, varying from 1 to 4 miles wide, that extends north for 22 miles into Grand Traverse Bay, separating the Bay's East Arm from its West Arm. While driving on M-37 at the peninsula's narrowest point, you can look to your right and to your left from the road's high ground and see the sparkling waters of both the East and West Arms. Visitors can also enjoy themselves at the peninsula's award-winning wineries, bed & breakfasts, and farm markets. The Mission Point Lighthouse, built in 1870, is located at the northern tip of the peninsula. The park built around the lighthouse features historic exhibits, public beaches, and hiking & ski trails.

Located a 15-minute drive southwest of Traverse City is the Interlochen Center for the Arts. Interlochen is one of the USA's premier training grounds for young (from 8 years old to post-graduate) musicians, artists, writers, dancers and actors. Students come from all 50 states and from over 40 countries around the world to experience and learn at Interlochen. The public is welcome to the 750 presentations (musical concerts, art exhibits, theater and dance productions) put on each year by the students. Besides the world-class education and life-long friends made, the students' environment is wonderful, too, with its rustic cabins nestled among the pines and between two lakes.

Today the tourism industry begun by Perry Hannah is the biggest economic driver for the area. Folks flock to Traverse City for fun including the National Cherry Festival, an 8-day event held each year in July, the T.C. Film Festival, a 6-day late-July gathering featuring the best in independent films (attracting over 100,000 folks), strolling the revitalized beauty of Downtown Front Street (Victorian buildings, shops, restaurants, galleries, bookstores) and, of course, enjoying paddling, swimming, tubing, skiing and sailing on the Boardman River and Grand Traverse Bay.

Area camping: the Traverse City State Park is located 2 miles east of downtown along a quarter-mile of Grand Traverse Bay's sandy beach. The park's 343 campsites lie within 47 wooded acres. The address is 1132 US31 N in Traverse City, phone (231) 922-5270.

THE TAVERN: PEEGEO'S

My publisher's preferred tavern and pizzeria… comments from other friends ("it's my favorite!")... the Internet reviews ("second to none", "great atmosphere", "best pizza hands down in Northern Michigan", "staff always friendly")… all told me that I need to go to Peegeo's. And then the clincher, as I pulled up to the front of the bar, there it hits me, the sign that reads, "Everyday - Pabst on tap, $1.50 a draft, $5 a 60 oz pitcher".

Peegeo's location is a really nice middle of nowhere. It is 20 minutes southeast of Traverse City and in the country on the north side of High Lake. When the weather's agreeable, there are 8 picnic tables for outdoor dining and imbibing.

Upon entering, you're reminded of Aubree's in Ypsilanti's Depot Town in its cool and comfortable darkness, the perfect amount of lighting for a tavern. The hot popcorn machine before you hit your seat is a nice touch. The backroom's classic old booths have great looking stained glass behind both booth benches. As nice as those classic booths are, you'll want to leave your booth to belly up to the bar, an area of Peegeo's that just draws you in. Maggie said that the cool-looking lights above the bar are "autumn globe pendant style lights" (exactly what I was thinking). To quote Maggie further, "Peegeo's is a good-for-getting-off-of-the-river kinda bar". You can see why I married her.

"Mmm, oh yeah" was the initial response after biting into a Peegeo's Angus Burger followed by, "<u>THIS</u> is a bar burger!" Our burgers were done to perfection.

As good as the burgers were, we had to try the pizza (winner of "Traverse Magazine's People's Choice Award"). We ordered "Mike's Sicilian", the favorite of both waitri working during our visit, a 12" square deep dish baked with garlic butter, Italian spices, a sprinkle of Romano cheese,

and your choice of two toppings. A good pizza holds up well over time, and this one was excellent at the bar and just as outstanding the next morning.

The Leinenkugel sign over the men's room door (wise advertising location) reminded me to check what Peegeo's had on tap. The draft selections were a fine assortment including Pabst Blue Ribbon, Wild Bill's Draft Root Beer, No. 9 Magic Hat, Labatt's Blue, Red Sky, Sam Adams, Octoberfest, and Bud Light.

"Peegeo's Legend" from the back of their menu: *Perry Hannah once owned most of the surrounding woods and lakes, one of Traverse City's founding fathers, who acquired the land for the purpose of removing timber. The land became popular with recreational users beginning in the late-*

1800s (so the timber remains). In this corner of Northern Michigan, as well as at Peegeo's, you're a visitor only once, thereafter you return as a prized friend. Signed, George & Susan VanKersen

Gordie Howe ate here in 1993. Under a glass frame is a Peegeo's Red Wings jersey, a photo of Gordie signing autographs at Peegeo's, and a Gordie signed hockey stick and puck. If George and Susan are looking for a future ad campaign theme, they may want to consider: *Peegeo's: " If it's good enough for Gordie Howe…"*

Peegeo's is located at 525 High Lake Road in Traverse City, phone (231) 941-0313.

Sources: Traverse Area Paddle Club, Michigan Department of Natural Resources and Environment, Michigan Paddlesports Directory, "Let's Fly Backward" by Al Barnes, Traverse City Record-Eagle, www.visittraversecity.com

CEDAR RIVER
Gladwin MI
Trip 5 miles
1 hour & 47 minutes

Beginner Ability

Livery: Cedar River Canoe Trips, corner of M61 & M30 (on the Tittabawassee River), Gladwin MI 48624; (989) 387-8658, www. gladwinboatrental.com. Owner Frank Stanislovatis. Frank services both the Cedar River and the Tittabawassee River.

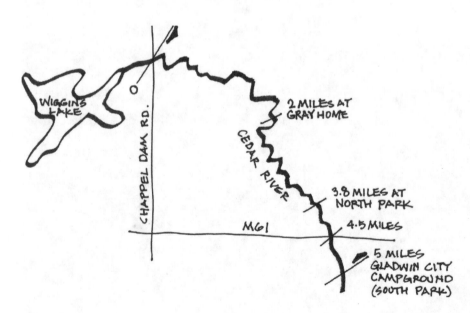

SOUNDTRACK:
Beer Barrel Polka – Cedar River Brass Quintet, Let's Dance – Ramones, Driver's Seat – Sniff 'n the Tears, Sic' Em On a Chicken – Zac Brown Band, Sun Is Still Shining – Moody Blues

RIVER QUOTE...
Ron: "There's a pedestrian bridge ahead. I don't mean to say that it's average"

MILES:
164 mi NW of Detroit, 132 mi NE of Grand Rapids, 138 mi South of Mackinaw City, 266 SE of Christmas, 398 mi NE of Milwaukee

THE BACKGROUND: CEDAR RIVER

The Cedar River has its headwaters in the center of Michigan's Lower Peninsula, just east of Harrison and 30 miles directly north of Mount Pleasant. From there, the river travels east to Wiggins Lake, located northwest of Gladwin. The Cedar River flows down from Wiggins Lake, meandering in a southeasterly direction, to Gladwin. At Gladwin, the river bends almost straight south heading to a rendezvous with the town of Beaverton. In Beaverton, the Cedar River completes its 40 mile journey as it empties into Ross Lake and the Tobacco River.

The section of the Cedar River covered in this chapter begins downstream from Wiggins Lake, launching just a few minutes beyond the dam at Chapel Dam Road. The put in at Chapel Dam Road is on private land and should be coordinated – whether you're using your own canoe/kayak or not – through Frank and the Cedar River Canoe Trips livery.

The paddle concludes on the sandy beach at the Gladwin City Campground (also known as South Park). The 5 mile trip usually takes 2 hours to complete. The trip for this book was taken in high water springtime conditions, resulting in a faster time of about one hour and 45 minutes.

The Cedar is a crystal-clear, shallow stream, averaging a depth of 1' to 3' and a width of 15' to 30'. This is a delightful little river with occasional rapids runs, beginner-friendly and fun for all. Fishing is good on the river for trout and smallmouth bass.

Crack Researchers paddling the Cedar River in April were Kenny Umphrey, Chris Weaks, Ron Swiecki, Jeff Cripe, Vicki Schroeder, Nadia Holyk, Jeff Vallender, Joyce Broka, and Doc.

THE RIVER: PADDLING THE CEDAR

Launch north of M61 where Chapel Dam Road crosses the Cedar River. The access is at the dock on the northwest corner of the bridge. Put in at the dock 30' upstream from the bridge. As you begin, the river is 25' wide and 1' deep.

.5 mi/11 min: as the Cedar bends right, on the left shore is Mike Grant's 10-acre farm. Mike has been known to welcome paddlers to use his picnic tables and outhouse.

.8 mi/20 min: after a left river bend, a 100' riffle run leads to a nice break spot on the left bank beach.

1 mile/24 min: when you paddle past the 20' tall bluffs on the right, you're exactly one mile into the trip. Two minutes downstream, a beautiful green-roofed log home lies on the left bank. Along the river in front of the house is a stone seawall. Above the stone seawall is a wall of railroad ties. Carved into a graveyard headstone near the waterline is "Clara M, 1931 – " (with no end date, the fun continues).

Fellow paddler Jeff Vallender grew up nearby and tells us that the land through which the Cedar flows today was all swamp until drained in the 1800s to allow for farming.

1.5 mi/37 min: whitewater, light class 1 rapids, precedes private property on the left, a two-tiered, long expanse of green.

1.7 mi/42 min: there's a brief whitewater run at a 3-wheeler crossing. Two minutes downstream, a very loud spring rolls down the hill on your left.

2 mi/47 min: the gray home on the left marks the end of a great class 1 rapids run, a 1/10th of a mile long whitewater adventure. Beyond the gray home lie a midstream island and a tall left bank bluff.

2.6 mi/1 hour: in the middle of the Cedar River, the 12' bottom of an uprooted tree faces you.

3 mi/1 hr 8 min: the dock to nowhere is on the left, followed by 3 bends of light riffles.

3.3 mi/1 hr 10 min: on the left shore is a series of sandy bluffs.

3.5 mi/1 hr 18 min: float beneath the power lines as the river bends left. The 50' tall bluff on the right is populated by tall, thin birch trees.

3.8 mi/1 hr 23 min: "North Park" is on the left. 2 minutes downstream, the small dune on the right is preceded by a shallow creek merging from the left.

North Park is the north starting point of the Cedar Riverwalk walking trail. Via pedestrian bridge crossings, the walking trail runs alternately along the left and right riverbanks. The south end of the walking trail is at the Gladwin City Park, where today's paddling trip ends.

4.2 mi/1 hr 30 min: paddle below power lines near the 12' tall sandy banks on the right. Beyond the left shore are private residences and rental homes. 4 minutes downstream you pass beneath a pedestrian bridge along the Cedar Riverwalk trail.

4.5 mi/1 hr 38 min: canoe and kayak below the back-to-back bridges of M61 and the Riverwalk trail. "Riverwalk Place" is just past the two bridges and on the left.

5 miles/1 hour 47 minutes: you're in! Take out at the Gladwin City Campground (South Park) sandy beach on the left shore.

THE TOWN: GLADWIN

Detroit Tigers local radio affiliate: WSGW 790AM

Cedar was the original name of the town of Gladwin - until it was discovered that there was already a town in Michigan named Cedar. 1883 was the year that Cedar was renamed Gladwin in honor of British Major Henry Gladwin. Major Gladwin gained fame when, in 1763, he was in charge of the only Midwest fort (Fort Detroit) that was successfully defended against the attacks of the warriors under Chief Pontiac. A portrait of Major Gladwin is displayed in the town's courthouse.

Before the arrival of the Europeans, the area was populated by the Sauk, Menominee and Ojibway tribes. The first settlers in Gladwin County arrived here by canoe (timelessly the best way to travel) in 1861 when Marvel Secord and his family paddled to this area on the Tittabawassee River. Marvel and his son Jerome constructed one of the first area buildings, a hunting lodge on the Tittabawassee in what is now Gladwin. In 1879, Marvel Secord was elected Supervisor of Cedar. Nearby Secord Township is named after Marvel. He is buried in Gladwin's Ridge Cemetery.

The original location of the town was in dispute in the 1870s. There were two original settlements, one at the first Chapel Dam (near the launch site of this chapter's Cedar River trip) and a second one in Cedar (where the Gladwin Courthouse sits today). The dispute was decided when a fire of *unknown origin* wiped out the Chapel Dam hamlet.

The cutting of the area's plentiful white pine forests

began in the 1870s when lumber camps were established in and around Cedar. By 1878, the lumber business was served in Cedar by the opening of 3 hotels and 14 saloons. A fire in 1900 destroyed many of the buildings in (what was by now called) Gladwin's business district. The loss was valued at a then staggering $100,000. The ruined wooden structures were replaced with brick buildings, many still standing in downtown Gladwin today.

The fabulous rivers and lakes in the Gladwin area provide plenty of opportunities for fishing, boating, canoeing and kayaking. 473 miles of streams and rivers include fun paddling on the Cedar, Sugar, Tobacco, Molasses and Tittabawassee rivers. Contributing to the good times on the water are over 50 nearby lakes. Covering one-quarter of Gladwin County is the Tittabawassee State Forest where you can hike, hunt and snowmobile.

Kenny's interpretation of livery owner Frank's business philosophy sums up what awaits you in Gladwin, formerly Cedar, "If you don't laugh here, you get your money back".

Area camping: available right on the Cedar at the end point of today's river trip is the Gladwin City Campground at South Park. The campground has 61 sites with electricity, fire rings and showers. It also features picnic areas, a playground, tennis courts and hiking trails. Right in downtown Gladwin, the campground is within walking distance of all the businesses in town including 2 minutes from the very cool Riverwalk Complex which overlooks the Cedar River. Make reservations at (989) 426-8126 or www.gladwin.org.

THE TAVERN: WOODEN SHOE BAR

The number of taverns in Michigan that you can paddle right up to seem to be endless. Add the Wooden Shoe to this wonderful list. The Shoe is located on the east bank of the Tittabawassee River, about 5 minutes east of downtown Gladwin on M61.

The father & son owners of the Wooden Shoe are Chris & Tim Helms. They do a fine job taking advantage of the bar's location by making it accessible 'n attractive. Getting from the river to the tavern is easy via the Wooden Shoe's boat ramp and multiple docking sites on the water. As you float by the bar, the look pulls you in. There is a great deck along the river, spacious and with its own tiki bar and adjacent sand volleyball courts.

Inside at the Wooden Shoe you'll find 3 pool tables and a big dance floor (you can dance to live music on the weekends). The 12' long kayak suspended from the ceiling is a nice touch.

Spending a night singing along to their juke box, drinking beer, chowing a Shoe burger, playing euchre, and watching the Tigers has all the makings of a real nice evening.

The Wooden Shoe Tavern is located at 247 E. M61 in Gladwin, phone (989) 397-8815. The bar sits on the east bank of the Tittabawassee River.

Sources: Frank Stanislovatis, Jeff Vallender, Gladwin Library staff, Gladwin County First Settler Centennial 1861-1961 by Bernice Walker Ritchie, Gladwin County Chamber of Commerce, Wah Cruice

CLINTON RIVER
Utica MI
Trip 4.6 miles
1 hour & 26 minutes

Veteran Ability

Livery: Clinton River Canoe & Kayak Rentals (also known as Outdoor Escorts, LLC), 916 Highlander, Lake Orion MI 48362, (248) 421-3445 and (248) 252-8229, www.outdoorescorts.com. Owners Jerry & Renee Reis.

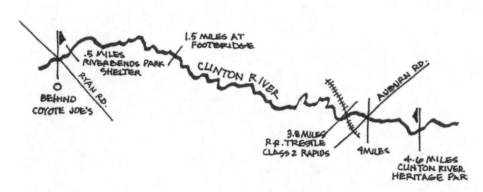

SOUNDTRACK: Wipeout – the Surfaris, Rochester River – Rockin Foo, East Bound & Down – Jerry Reed, Train to Nowhere – Savoy Brown, 7 Months 39 Days – Hank Williams III

RIVER QUOTE...
Spencer: "We need to do this more often!"

MILES: 18 mi North of Detroit, 160 mi East of Grand Rapids, 272 mi SE of Mackinaw City, 400 mi SE of Christmas, 390 mi East of Milwaukee

THE BACKGROUND: CLINTON RIVER

From its headwaters near Pontiac, the Clinton River winds east for 80 miles until it flows into Lake St. Clair east of Mt. Clemens. Along the way, the Clinton meanders through Auburn Hills, Rochester Hills, Rochester, Shelby Township, Utica, Sterling Heights, Clinton Township, Mt. Clemens, and Harrison Township.

Recreational activity on the Clinton has increased several times over since the late-2000s. In 2009, Jerry and Renee Reis opened their livery service, Clinton River Canoe & Kayak Rentals. Since 2009, working with his friend Dale Goolsby and others, Jerry has cleared long stretches of the river, stretches previously so clogged with debris as to be rendered unusable to canoe and kayak. Arm these guys with chain saws, winches and ropes and you get a river that's now safe for paddling fun!

Jerry and crew have opened up a series of one and two-hour (combine these for a longer stay on the river) paddling trips on the Clinton, beginning from the Squirrel Road access in Auburn Hills downstream to the canoe landing (opened 2011) at Heritage Park in Utica. The skill levels needed to paddle the trips on the Squirrel Road to Heritage Park section of the Clinton ranges from "beginner-friendly" to "experienced paddlers only!"

The wildest section (i.e. high skill level required) of the Clinton runs through Rochester Hills and Rochester, between Livernois and 2nd Street. Jerry refers to this as "the run for the brave". Whether beginner or brave, Jerry and Renee will help make your day an enjoyable one by matching the paddling skills of your group with the appropriate section of the river.

The Clinton River trip outlined in this chapter is an extremely fun 90 minute paddle:

- 40% of our boats flipped over.
- 100% of our paddlers LOVED the trip!

We launched in Shelby Township on Ryan Road behind Coyote Joe's Bar and took out at the Heritage Park canoe landing in Utica. This trip earned a degree of difficulty rating of "Veteran" due to the strong current, occasionally pulling you towards river obstructions, class 1 and 2 rapids, and frequent deadfall (to keep it fun, Jerry had to leave SOME stuff in the river). You paddle beneath a beautiful canopy of trees for much of the float, very cooling on a hot summer day. Multiple stone and dirt beaches along the way provide great swimming & get out 'n stretch your legs break locations.

Owning a canoe and kayak livery brings smiles everyday to Jerry and Renee, in part because of the questions asked by customers: did you know there are rocks in the river? (for "rocks" you may substitute logs, spiders, or snakes) and who do we contact to have them taken care of? Are we going to get wet? Which way do we go? One gentleman was stuck on a log and called Jerry to come and get him unstuck. In water 16" deep. This customer decided not to wait for Jerry and called 911. Amazingly, his call was not considered a 911 priority and they did not come and rescue him. He did make it back to the dock and wanted a refund – and then came back next week with 6 friends for more kayaking (no rescue call this time, maybe that's what the friends were brought along for).

As you read over the river recap, note that the river was running 6" above its normal stage and close to its usual speed. With so many impervious surfaces just beyond its river banks, the Clinton, like the Rouge, is one of Michigan's fastest flooding rivers and is strongly impacted by heavy rains. As an example, only 4 days before our paddle the river was 5' (feet, not inches) higher from recent rains and the tall logjam that a group shot was taken at was underwater 4 days prior. Call the Clinton River Canoe & Kayak Rentals for the most up-to-date water levels.

Fishermen on the Clinton have caught rainbow, steelhead, bass, walleye, pike, catfish, suckers, creek chubs and even sturgeon.

Crack researchers on the Clinton at the start of August were Kathy, John & Katrina Harcourt, Nola Mayfield, Dale Froriep, Gilda Weaks, Gomie Carroll, Jenny Brandies, Chris, Madelynn & Gus Weaks, Vid Marvin, Ron, Tina & Ronnie Jr. Swiecki, Vicki Schroeder, Nadia Holyk, Al & Peggy Van Kerckhove, Jeff Vallender, Tim Patrick, Jimmy & Spencer Vollmers, Dale Kittendorf, Jesse Changa, Paula Brown, Andy Kocembo, Dylan Welch, Dale Goolsby, Jerry, Renee, Sam &

Shaun Reis, Maggie & Doc.

Invaluable logistics support was provided by John "J bro" Pienta.

THE RIVER: PADDLING THE CLINTON

Launch in Shelby Township behind Coyote Joe's Bar, on Ryan Road south of 22 Mile, beginning a 4 and a half mile journey that will end at Heritage Park in Utica. Much of this trip is through a riverbed 1' to 2' deep and 20' wide. You'll be paddling through *River Bends Park* for the first 3.5 miles of the journey.

.4 mi/8 min: a 4' tall debris field blocks the right side of the river. Just beyond is a large stone island. Very fast water flows around both sides of the island.

.5 mi/11 min: on the right shore is a River Bends Park shelter with restrooms.

During this first half mile, through the class 1 rapids are strong currents that must be fought to avoid being pulled into river obstructions.

.8 mi/18 min: a fast-moving creek rolls in from the right.

1 mi/24 min: the small island right of midstream makes for a great break spot and swimming hole, accessible on either side.

2 minutes downstream from this quaint little island, stay sharp...

1.1 mi/26 min: **beware!** Sticking 2' above the water line (in these "normal" depth conditions) is a midstream support post of an abandoned pedestrian bridge. The river's current tries to slam you into this newly-christen Al & Peggy post, so be on your toes.

1.5 mi/33 min: float beneath a red footbridge. This is part of a walking trail that takes folks from Stony Creek, at 23 Mile Road & M53, to Metro Beach at Lake St. Clair.

2 minutes downstream is a great 100 yard long class 1 rapids run.

1.7 mi/37 min: as the Clinton River bends right there is a fine stone beach on the right.

2 mi/43 min: left of midstream is a heavily wooded stone & dirt island, passable either left or right. Just downstream from the island are brief class 2 rapids that take you into a longer class 1 run.

2.2 mi/47 min: great break island is right of midstream, another in a series of fine stone & dirt islands. 1 minute downstream, a big creek merges left.

3.3 mi/1 hr 5 min: small island lies midstream 2 minutes before you float beneath power lines.

3.6 mi/1 hr 10 min: along the right bluff precariously sits abandoned railroad tracks.

3.8 mi/1 hr 12 min: **Wee-Ha!** Paddle below a railroad trestle and into some brief but spectacular class 2 rapids. Great fun!

4 mi/1 hr 18 min: as you float beneath the Auburn Road Bridge, Muldoon's Bar is 200' to your left, beyond the big riverside clock.

2 minutes past Auburn Road you paddle under M59. It is two more minutes to the green pedestrian bridge.

4.6 miles/1 hour 27 minutes: you're in! The Heritage Park canoe landing is on your left.

THE TOWN: UTICA

Detroit Tigers local radio affiliate: WXYT 97.1FM & 1270AM

Utica is a small town of just under two square miles located in Macomb County. A Utica resident with a hankering for a Lafayette or an American Coney Island would have an 18-mile drive almost perfectly straight south to the downtown Detroit corner of Lafayette and Michigan Avenues.

It was in 1817 that the first person took up residence in Utica. Thomas Squire relocated from his Mount Clemens home, traveling west along the Clinton River, building his cabin where two Indian trails met the riverside high ground. The young settlement was referred to by the names Hog's Hollow or McDougalville or, most often, Harlow.

and to the folks of Utica.

Could Michigan emulate the success of New York's Erie Canal? From Lake St. Clair, the Clinton River itself would be used through Mt. Clemens to the ghost town of Frederick, just SW of Mt. Clemens at the merger of the Clinton River & the North Branch of the Clinton, where today Canal Road meets Clinton River Road. The digging for the canal began on July 20, 1838 in Frederick, heading west to Utica, alongside what is today Canal Road. An estimated 200 canal miles would be dug from Frederick to Allegan County, from there using the Kalamazoo River as the connection to Lake Michigan.

By 1843 excavation had only reached the area of today's Yates Cider Mill in Rochester when

Harlow, platted in 1829 by Joseph Snead, soon began to attract a large number of settlers from the state of New York. These Yankees changed the name of the town from Harlow to Utica in honor of the city with the same name in their home state (New York settlers did the same for Utica's neighboring towns of Rochester and Troy).

The big draw to Utica for many migrating from the east coast was the proposed *Clinton-Kalamazoo Canal*. Plans for this canal were announced in 1837, the year that Michigan achieved statehood. The Clinton-Kalamazoo Canal would serve as a water highway that could transport goods and people across southern Michigan from Lake St. Clair to Lake Michigan, a huge boost to the economy of the young state,

the money ran out. A historical marker notes the spot. In 5 years, only 13 of the proposed 200 miles had been dug. The possibility of resurrecting the canal died with the coming of the railroads. Today, remains of the canal can be seen along Canal Road between Clinton River Road and Utica, and at 3 locations in Shelby Township (1) along the nature trail in River Bends Park, (2) on 22 Mile Road just west of Shelby Road and (3) on Ryan Road north of 22 Mile.

Area camping: Addison Oaks County Park is the nearest campground to the Clinton River. This 1,140 acre park with lakes and ponds is north 30 minutes (19 miles) from

Utica's Heritage Park. Addison has individual & group sites with full hookups, cabins for rent, swimming, trails for hiking and biking, and picnic shelters. To get there from the canoe landing at Heritage Park, take M59 west to Rochester Road then north to Romeo Road. Turn left on Romeo (32 Mile Road). Addison is two miles away. Their address is 1480 West Romeo Road in Leonard MI 48367, phone (248) 693-2432, and website is www.destinationoakland.com.

THE TAVERN: MULDOON'S

Muldoon's is housed in a building constructed over 100 years ago, and is within Utica's designated Historic District, centered on Auburn Road and Cass Avenue. Most of these buildings can be dated back to the 1906 rebuilding of the town, after widespread fires in 1905 and 1906 wiped out many residences and most of the business district.

The pub's location is very convenient to this Clinton River trip, only 5 walking minutes north of the Heritage Park canoe landing take out.

"Woo!" says Maggie about the Cuervo. It sounded like a good "Woo!" This fine old Irish Tavern did have room for all 35 of us after our day on the Clinton. We descended on the bar at 330PM on a Monday afternoon, a larger crowd than they're used to at that time of day. The food orders were filled amazingly fast, but with a few mistakes (think of the auto assembly line scenes near the end of the movie "Gung Ho").

We found the homemade pizza excellent and its crust done to perfection. Muldoon's sandwiches received unanimous approval from everyone in our group who ordered them.

This century-old building was originally a blacksmith shop. In recent years, it has been operated as a pub under the names Squat 'n Gobble, Old Towne Café, and Cactus Jack's.

It became Muldoon's in November of 2008.

Inside the tavern are big screen TVs, 2 dart boards, a pool table, a juke box, and a framed Detroit News front page from December 6, 1933 with the headline "Prohibition Is Out!" (as a side note, the arguably bigger news that month was that the Tigers signed Mickey "Iron Mike" Cochrane as their playing manager; first World Championship, here we come!).

Outdoors at Muldoon's has its own stocked bar, a great tiki bar, and a patio with circular brick fire pits and heating towers for nippy evenings.

Muldoon's, although very Irish, tips their hat to Germany by stocking Pabst Blue Ribbon Beer. Also, as this is being written Pabst is Muldoon's "Beer of the Month". Really, isn't it always?

Muldoon's is located at 7636 Auburn Road in Utica MI 48317. They are a 5-minute walk north from Heritage Park, 1 block north and 2 blocks west of Van Dyke. Phone (586) 739-6946. Check out their website at www. muldoonstavern.com.

BONUS TAVERN: PAINT CREEK

The original Clinton River plan was to paddle the two hours ending at Yates Cider Mill in Rochester Hills. However, late in the summer the water on this stretch of the Clinton was too low to float a canoe (a reminder why it's always good to check current conditions with the livery beforehand). For the trip ending at Yates, I sought input on area taverns from a local resident who would know of such things, Ernie Harwell's partner behind the mike, and the man with the golden voice, Paul Carey. Here was Paul's suggestion…

Nothing in the immediate vicinity of Yates Cider Mill, but the likeliest bet would be the Paint Creek Tavern in downtown Rochester. It's on the west side of Main Street (Rochester Road) perched on the south side of Paint Creek. Haven't been there for a couple of years, but I know that when the weather is good, you can eat and drink out alongside the creek. It's at 613 N. Main and the phone number is 248-656-2322. Have fun and don't have too many Pfeiffers. Paul

Paul made the Paint Creek Tavern sound like a place that would be fun to visit, just like he made Tiger Stadium sound for lo those many wonderful years of broadcasting along side Ernie. But, since Paul had not been at the tavern in a couple of years, and understanding the importance of imparting the most up-to-date information to this book's readers, a trip to the tavern was arranged for this publication by Paul, Joe Sayers, Tim Patrick and Doc.

We found that both indoors and outdoors the PCT is, as Paul's note had suggested it would be, an inviting place to be…

Inside, you're in a cozy room the size of a railroad car. 42 beers are on tap – an amazing amount in such a small space – including Pabst Blue Ribbon beer. The wait staff was on- their-toes excellent, and the regulars were smiling, friendly, and very welcoming to visitors.

Outside, you're seated right alongside the fast flowing Paint Creek, a tributary to the Clinton River. What a great view from the deck there is of this delightful little stream. The great view was enhanced by the tasty burgers and ham 'n cheese sandwiches we ate.

It should be noted that Paint Creek flows south from the bar until, shortly after passing beneath 2nd Street, it merges with the Clinton River. Between the tavern and the Clinton River, the creek is shallow and there is a partially-removed dam in downtown Rochester that forms a paddling obstruction. During springtime's elevated water levels, the shallow bottom is not an issue and the water may be high enough to allow you to work your way around dam remnants. You can scout the area of the dam, and decide whether the water is deep enough to paddle through, by parking at the Royal Park Hotel and taking a 3-minute walk south along the Paint Creek Trail.

The day of our visit,

the Tigers defeated that Texas Rangers in game 5 of the American League Championship Series. Now, we cannot guarantee a Tiger playoff victory if you visit the Paint Creek Tavern, but we can guarantee a fine time.

Check out the bar's website at www.paintcreektavern.com.

Sources: www.cityofutica.org, Jerry Reis, Shelby Township Historical Committee, Michigan Historical markers, Paul Carey

CROCKERY CREEK

Spoonville MI
Trip 4.3 miles
1 hour & 56 minutes

Intermediate Ability

Livery: Lakeshore Kayak Rental, 14023 Green Street (in Felix's Marina), Grand Haven MI 49417; (616) 566-1325, www. lakeshorekayakrental.com. Owners - Karen and Bob Chapel. Lakeshore also services the Grand River and the Pigeon River.

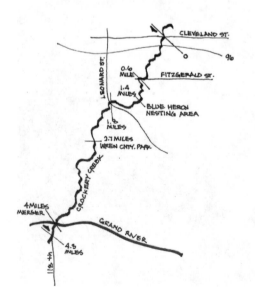

SOUNDTRACK: Up On Cripple Creek – the Band, Hot Smoke & Sassafrass – Bubble Puppy, Opus One – Tommy Dorsey, Looking At You – MC5, Don't Lie Buddy – Lead Belly & Josh White

RIVER QUOTE...

Kenny: "I'd rather be cozy than have my cheeks rosy – both sets of cheeks"

MILES: 192 mi West of Detroit, 34 mi West of Grand Rapids, 263 mi SW of Mackinaw City, 391 mi South of Christmas, 263 mi East of Milwaukee

THE BACKGROUND: CROCKERY CREEK

Crockery Creek offers a great wildlife viewing paddling adventure to visiting kayakers and canoers. This pretty and secluded little stream begins about 5 driving minutes north of the town of Nunica and 15 minutes east of the Lake Michigan shoreline town of Grand Haven. From start to finish, Crockery Creek flows south for 10 miles.

The trip outlined in this chapter launches a few feet northeast of I96 at exit 10 / Nunica. From there you paddle the Creek's final 4 miles until it empties into the mighty

Grand River. You find yourself meandering down made-in-Michigan bayou country, paddling beneath and around leaning branches, midstream deadwood and plenty of trees jutting out of the water (some, and only some, of the bayou feel was due to the early-Spring high water levels encountered

by the crack research team). The frequency of obstructions make this an enjoyable paddling challenge and not well-suited for beginners.

Crockery Creek wildlife included a herd of at least 30 deer stampeding ahead of us. The sound of their pounding hooves echoed through the woods as the deer were visible in spectacular flashes through the trees, treating our group to a beautiful sight & sound. The experience was akin to a scene from *Lonesome Dove* with Captain Call, Augustus and the boys driving a herd of horses across the prairie. We floated beneath a grouping of 23 Blue Heron nests in the trees, 50' or so above the water line. Big birds and big nests! While some

of the birds stayed in the nests, others took to the sky above squawking their distaste for our intrusion into their lives. It was quite a sight. Since Blue Herons use the same nests for several years at a time, a viewing treat such as this can be enjoyed many times over. Sandhill cranes, ducks and geese were seen in large numbers. Eagle sightings are also reputed to happen frequently along Crockery Creek.

There has been good success fishing Crockery Creek for brown trout and steelhead.

Crack researchers paddling Crockery Creek on May 1st, after several rainy days raised the creek level, were Kenny, Brian & Aubrey Umphrey, Mister P Pienta, and Doc Fletcher.

THE RIVER: PADDLING CROCKERY CREEK

Launch on the south side of Nunica along Cleveland Street and the northern edge of I-96. This launch site is just a quarter mile northeast of exit 10 at I-96. The best entry point here is on the east side of the river.

In summer "normal" water levels, Crockery Creek runs about 5' to 6' deep. In seasonal spring high water, you're paddling at depths between 8' to 10'. The river width at launch is 25'. You immediately float beneath the bridges at Cleveland St. and I-96.

.4 mi/14 min: the creek splits into two bodies of water; the left split veers perpendicular to the main body of the creek creating the upstream end of an island. Two additional river splits to the left occur in the next 5 minutes. For the deeper water, take the right splits.

.5 mi/17 min: at a left river bend, the current picks up speed dramatically; there is plenty of deadwood and leaning trees to contend with – come in slowly.

.6 mi/20 min: paddle below the Fitzgerald Street Bridge.

Crockery Creek is proving to be great fun! Hanging branches are everywhere, trees lean in from both riverbanks at a 45 degree angle, and there is frequent deadwood that you have to maneuver your way through and around.

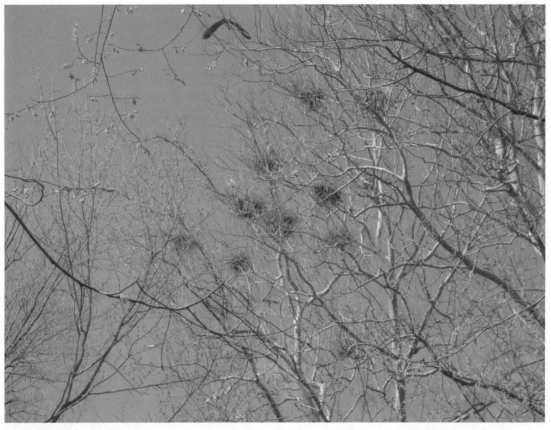

Tributary streams merge, the river splits again and again, and little alcoves lie adjacent to the river. You can tell that not too many folks paddle through here. The sweet seclusion is broken by a thundering herd of deer visible through the trees and along the right shore just ahead of us.

1 mi/33 min: a river finger breaks off to the right, forming the upstream end of an island.

1.4 mi/43 min: in the trees 50' above the water line, 23 nests belonging to Blue Herons are counted. When these birds are getting ready to lay their eggs, the ideal location is chosen. The males then travel to gather twigs and branches for the females who weave the twigs and branches into a nest. Blue Heron nests may be found anywhere from 20' to 100' above the river or shoreline.

1.5 mi/46 min: after passing by a home on the left shore, a fallen log lies across & above the river straddling both the right and left banks. In the seasonal high water, there is 3' of paddling clearance from the river surface to the bottom of the log.

1.8 mi/55 min: canoe and kayak beneath the Leonard Street Bridge. Once past the bridge, a finger of the river splits to the left while the main body of the water flows right.

Beginning just past the Leonard Street Bridge, the early-May high water creates a flooded plain that you paddle through. It's hard to tell how much of this flooded plain exist during "normal" water levels.

1.9 mi/58 min: with homes and barns beyond the right shore, a sign posted on a left bank tree tells you that you have ventured past the park boundary. This park is the "Crockery Creek Natural Area", a 331 acre natural area that you paddle on the western edge of for the next 2 river miles, all the way until you merge from the Creek into the Grand River. The natural area is a breeding ground for bald eagles, sandhill cranes, river otters, red-headed woodpeckers and serves as a staging area for many migratory birds.

2.2 mi/1 hr 6 min: beyond the bayou to your right, a home sits on a 30' high bluff as the river takes a bend to the left.

Cranes, geese and herons are all around us!

2.5 mi/1 hr 15 min: an abandoned Three Stooges-style bathtub is in the woods to your left (some landmarks are more permanent in nature then others).

2.7 mi/1 hr 20 min: Wren County Park is on the left bluff.

3 mi/1 hr 30 min: coming down a hill and towards the river, a crevice cuts through the land on your right.

Due to the very high seasonal water level, it has become difficult to follow the river line as the creek has widened to

400'. The park boundary signs posted on trees sticking out of the river (trees usually on dry ground) are a helpful guide to keep you on the river path.

The maps tell us that there is a large creek merging from the left. It is impossible to differentiate the merging creek from Crockery Creek as they are together one sprawling body of water without boundaries.

4 mi/1 hr 56 min: Crockery Creek flows into the Grand River; here the Grand is 1/4 mile wide, flowing from left to right, on its way to a merger with Lake Michigan. The take-out at the 118th Street DNR access is across the Grand and slightly to the right.

4.25 miles/2 hours: you've crossed the Grand and you're in! Leave the Grand River at the boat ramp on its south shore. There is a rest room 10' to the left of the ramp.

THE TOWN:
THE GHOST TOWN OF
SPOONVILLE

Detroit Tigers local radio affiliate:
WBBL 107.3FM (Grand Haven)

Had you been paddling down Crockery Creek from the mid to the late 1800s, during the last few minutes on the approach to the Grand River you would have looked to your right and seen a prosperous community, one that has now completely disappeared. The name of this ghost community was Spoonville.

Located a few minutes south of the town of Nunica, Spoonville was a large settlement that sat on the watery crossroads of the west side of the rivermouth (ending) of Crockery Creek and the north bank of the Grand River.

Spoonville's origins sprang from a sawmill built here in 1856 by brothers John and Dan Spoon and their partners. The sawmill was located on the west side of what is now 120th Avenue, across the Grand from the present day marina.

The first homes in the young village were the mansions built by each of the brothers. Dan Spoon soon began to run a large farm in addition to his work at the sawmill. Two huge barns, the biggest in all of Ottawa County, were built to support the farming activities. The large number of workers required to operate the 848 acres of the farm and sawmill needed a place to live. By 1857 homes for the workers, a company store (the

type of place where Tennessee Ernie Ford owed his soul), a horse barn, blacksmith shop, tavern, an office building, and an unofficial post office were among the Spoonville structures.

Between the sawmill and the farm, business was so good that the Chicago & Michigan Lake Shore Railroad ran a rail line through Spoonville in 1870. This rail line ran from Benton Harbor north through Holland, crossing the Grand River at Spoonville on its way to Nunica and points north.

The forests feeding the sawmill were cut until they disappeared and sawmill operations came to a close in the 1880s. The Chicago & Michigan Railroad folks then decided to cease using the section of the rail running through Spoonville, but there was one problem with that decision: in 1870 the local community had signed a 99-year agreement with the railroad company to keep the rail line open through

town. In order to force the railroad to honor the agreement, local folks planned to obtain a court injunction. Knowing that this injunction would be obtained the following Monday, the rail company arranged to have the tracks dismantled under cover of darkness beginning at midnight Saturday. By the time that the injunction could be obtained from the court on Monday morning, the track had been removed.

What happened to the remainder of Spoonville? The bridge on which the railroad line ran stayed in place for a few years after the rail left until a fire finished it off. Although work at the sawmill was gone by the late-1800s, the farm started by Dan Spoon continued to operate successfully into the early 1900s. After the Spoon brothers passed away, the farm activities slowly ground to a halt as new owners began to sell off the land piece by piece. With no work, the Spoonville residents moved away and all of the town buildings were either dismantled and moved, torn down, or burned down by the mid-1900s.

Area camping: There is no camping at the Crockery Creek Natural Area. Camping is available 4 miles southeast of the Crockery Creek I96 exit 10 Nunica launch. On the north shore of the Grand River is the Conestoga Grand River Campground at 9720 Oriole Drive in Coopersville 49404, phone (616) 837-6323. From the launch site, take 112th Street south to Leonard St, turn left at Leonard and go to 96th Avenue. Turn right on 96th Ave to Oriole where you'll again turn right to Conestoga.

Conestoga has 81 sites along the river, a camp store, and hook ups for electric, water and sewer. Their website is www.conestogacampground.com.

THE TAVERN: TURK'S INN

Just a few hundred feet west of where this chapter's Crockery Creek trip launches, sitting alone but not forlorn, is the tavern known as Turk's Inn. Turk's Inn is a delightful place to visit and eat, the kind that makes you want to return again and again, as most visitors do. It is one of the oldest bar/restaurants in all of Ottawa County.

Turk Allison celebrated the 1933 lifting of Prohibition by opening Turk's Inn during that same year. Cozy, quirky, and charming, the tavern looks much the same today as it did in 1933. The original wood carvings, including a "T" in each booth, remain. Swinging doors leading into the bathrooms is a neat touch. The interior is beautifully dark and accented with some fine lighting. When Frances and Roger Holmes bought Turk's in the 1980s, they wisely maintained the tradition established by keeping the Turk's Inn name.

You'll find no beer on tap here, but you will find over 40 bottled beers, including Pabst, always a sure sign of quality. "Eat, Drink & Be Bloody Merry" is the inscription on a Turk's Inn shirt. More than once, Turk's has won the "Best Bloody Mary Championship" at the Spring Lake Heritage Festival.

Turk's food was a big winner with our crack research team. *The Rosie Burger* was a creation by the Inn's former cook Rosie, and it's a fine legacy that she left behind: the half-pound burger includes shaved ham, crisp bacon, melted cheese, tomato, mayo and onion. Oh yeah. The *Emerald Irish Salmon Salad* is not your usual salmon salad, coming with a very generous sized filet served on a bed of lettuce, grilled cabbage and onions, along with bacon crumbles, redskin potato and a hardboiled egg. Very tasty. But what disappeared the quickest from our table, a real tribute, was the basket of chicken wings.

Turk's is open 7 days a week, from 11AM on Monday through Friday, and earlier for breakfast on the weekend (7AM Saturday and 8AM Sunday). If you happen to be in Holland, you can visit their second location at 977 Butternut Drive, (616) 796-8558.

Turk's Inn is located at 11139 Cleveland Street in Nunica, I96 exit 10, phone (616) 837-7096. Their website is www.turks-inn.com

Sources: Karen & Bob Chapel, my.voyager.com,www. ghosttowns.com

FLINT RIVER
Flushing Mi
Trip 12.8 miles
2 hours & 26 minutes

Livery: Good Ol' Redbeard's, 114 E. Main Street, Flushing MI 48433, (810) 210-7602, www.goodoleredbeard.com. Owners Brent LaPonsey and Jim Tift.

Intermediate Ability

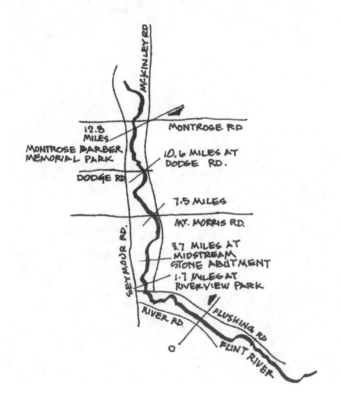

SOUNDTRACK: Luckenbach Texas – Pole Barn Rebels (PBRs), Riverboat Shuffle – Bix Beiderbecke, Five Feet High & Rising – Johnny Cash, The Sky is Crying – Elmore James, When the Music's Over – the Doors

RIVER QUOTE...
Teresa Salem: "The river is just so beautiful. It takes you away from your everyday life"

MILES: 77 mi NW of Detroit, 100 mi East of Grand Rapids, 220 mi SE of Mackinaw City, 350 mi SE of Christmas, 360 mi East of Milwaukee

THE BACKGROUND: FLINT RIVER

The Flint River begins its 75 mile journey near Columbiaville, a few miles northeast of Flint. From Columbiaville, it flows southwest to Flint then pivots to the northwest as it passes through Flushing and Montrose, working its way to a merger with the Shiawassee River in the Shiawassee National Wildlife Refuge near Saginaw.

This river will surprise you. If you asked most folks who had never paddled down the Flint what comes to mind when they think of the Flint River, there's a good chance that they'd say "urban", "industry", "polluted" and "why would you want to paddle down the Flint?" After canoeing and kayaking the 13 miles from Flushing to Montrose, they would likely say what we did, "delightful", "scenic", "rural", "memorable" and "how soon can I get back?"

Even on a cloudy day, the beauty of the Flint River was clear. You encounter forests of Trillium flowers, travel alongside geese and blue herons, pass frequent midstream

wooded islands, and paddle through rapids and by merging creeks. You'll float alongside the *River View Trail* and under pedestrian bridges that allow the Trail to wind from one riverbank to the other. Homes along the way were few, beautiful, unobtrusively playing a supporting role to the river. And then there's the river's health and clarity…

As recently as the mid-2000s, recreational use of the Flint was rare. The river's reputation was a poor one from the many factories that once lined and polluted the river. Since the late 1990s, the health of the river has undergone a wonderful metamorphosis due in large part to the efforts of the *Flint River Watershed Coalition*, formed in 1997. Pollution has been greatly minimized through the FRWC's activities. Coalition members meet with riverside residents and businesses, guiding them towards making better decisions on how they interact with the river and the entire watershed. The FRWC regularly organizes river cleanups and monitors and tests the water quality on an ongoing basis.

With a much healthier and surprisingly clear river, frequency of canoeing and kayaking the Flint has increased several times over since the late-2000s. The Flint River Watershed Coalition schedules paddling events during the year, encouraging people to get out on the water and enjoy the wonderful gift that the Flint River is. Check out the Coalition at http://flintriver.org/blog.

The section of the Flint River paddled for this chapter begins at Flushing's River Road access and ends 13 miles downstream at the Barber Park canoe landing in the town of Montrose. This is usually a 4 hour trip, but since we paddled in mid-May during the elevated water levels of springtime, a rainier than usual May at that, the result was a speedy run of just under 2 and a half hours. Through Flushing, the Flint River's usual cfps (cubic feet per second) is 400. During this mid-May paddle the cfps was 5,000 and it was the fastest the river's been on a May 18th since 1956 (I believe that Frank Lary beat the Yankees that day; the Hungarians didn't fare so well). We reached a maximum speed of 8.4 mph, averaging 5.3 mph.

The "normal" times (summer speeds) to each landmark from the River Road access start:
30 minutes to Riverview Park, 2.5 hours to Mt. Morris Road, 4 hours to Montrose ending.

Fishing on the Flint is good for carp, largemouth bass, catfish and walleye. The walleye fishing in Flushing is so good that the town has an annual festival to celebrate it. Go to www.flushingwalleye.com.

Crack research team members paddling the Flint River on May 18th included Greg Palinsky, Rebecca Fedewa, Teresa Salem, Dennis Bow, Jameson Carle, Joe Tobianski, Vicki Schroeder, Nadia Holyk, Gary "Mothman" Muir, Maggie and Doc.

THE RIVER: PADDLING THE FLINT

Launch in Flushing at the excellent canoe landing of the River Road Access, across the river from the Flushing Valley Golf Course. The river's average width on this mid-May paddle was 120' (normal 80') and the depth 7' to 12' (normal 1' to 6').

1.7 mi/18 min: sitting on a right bend of the river and on the right is *Riverview Park*, a beautiful park in downtown Flushing. In the distance behind Riverview Park is Good 'Ol Redbeard's livery.

2 mi/22 min: paddle under the Main Street Bridge. *River View Trail* is on the left shore as is, one minute downstream,

Johnny's Pour House tavern (not visible from the river).

2.5 mi/26 min: Cole Creek merges from the left. A wastewater plant is ahead on the left.

2.7 mi/28 min: on the right is *Flushing County Park* on a bluff 70' above the river. At the top of the bluff, the park's fence is visible from the river.

3 mi/31 min: paddle below a pedestrian bridge for the River View Trail. This takes people to and from the County Park on the right shore. The trail ends past the park at Carpenter Road.

3.2 mi/34 min: reach the upstream tip of a wooded island passable either left or right (the main body of the river flows left). Beyond is a 2nd wooded island left of midstream.

3.5 mi/36 min: ***great class 2 rapids fun!*** These are very active with standing waves breaking into some of our canoes and kayaks. A wild ride!

An old clay pit is beyond the tall right bank ridge and not visible from the river.

3.7 mi/39 min: ghost bridge… midstream is a stone abutment supporting nothing; it once supported a coal mining bridge. In the middle of the river are two islands 3 minutes apart.

4.2 mi/44 min: to the right is a beautiful sight, a forest of Trillium flowers.

4.8 mi/51 min: pass by back-to-back islands.

5.2 mi/55 min: on both sides of the river are fine looking homes including one sweet log cabin on the left.

5.3 mi/56 min: the river splits evenly right and left around a battleship-sized wooded island. It takes 4 minutes to reach the downstream tip of it. A smaller island follows.

6.6 mi/1 hr 10 min: a series of beautiful, oversized homes are on the right along McKinley Road.

7.5 mi/1 hr 20 min: paddle beneath the Mt. Morris Road Bridge.

7.7 mi/1 hr 23 min: on the right is a deck with a bench connecting the river to a walkway of the *Flushing Township Nature Park*.

8.3 mi/1 hr 30 min: on the right bank is a river access at the Nature Park.

10.3 mi/1 hr 56 min: fields of Trillium flowers are along the right shore; reach the upstream tip of a small wooded island with picnic table, a favorite break spot of the *Flint River Paddlers*.

10.6 mi/2 hrs: on the left, a path descends down a small hill towards the river; up the path 50' from the water is Dodge Road.

11 mi/2 hrs 5 min: an interesting visual: side-by-side islands allow equidistant room to paddle between or far left or far right.

11.5 mi/2 hrs 10 min: really nice run of rapids on a long straightaway; on a tall bluff is a great looking wooden home on the left shortly after the rapids begin. These rapids run for two full minutes, and at their end is a very large and wide island, passable right or left. This island is one-half mile long, a 7-minute paddle from start to finish (more time is required in slower "normal" conditions). At the end of the island are two very nice log cabins on the left.

12.8 miles/2 hours 26 minutes: you're in! Exit left at the Barber Memorial Park canoe landing in Montrose. The park has two floating docks at the river's edge (handicap accessible), a deck over the river with benches, restrooms, hiking and biking trails, kid's playscape, baseball diamond, shelter, and (for <u>very</u> early season paddlers) a sledding hill.

THE TOWN: FLUSHING

Detroit Tigers local radio affiliate
WTRX 1330AM

Flushing is fortunate to have so many concerned citizens passionate about the quality of life in the town and in maintaining the health of their Flint River. That passion is evident in the time & effort committed by groups like the Flushing River View Trail Committee, the Flint River Watershed Coalition, and the Flint Paddlers. Their actions and those of like-minded residents make Flushing a great place to live and to visit.

Flushing is a comfortable small town of about 8,000 folks that is a 15-minute drive northwest of Flint. Most of Flushing's southern border is formed by the Flint River. One of the town's jewels is Riverview Park, a great place to drive, walk, or paddle to (just under 2 miles into this chapter's Flint River trip). The park hosts free events throughout the year including "Art In The Park", "Movies In The Park" and the "Concerts In The Park" series in its band shell. In addition to all of the fun at Riverview Park, there's a long list of community events to keep you busy like the annual Walleye Festival (proceeds from which funded Flushing's new River Road access launch, this chapter's starting point), Harvest Festival, Fabulous 50s Festival (Summerfest), and the miles of candles of the Christmas Candlewalk.

The Flushing Farmer's Market weekly has fresh produce and fun eating like habanaro cheese burgers, mushroom and swiss brats, and apple cider slushies. Twilight Tuesdays offer summer nighttime live entertainment, giveaways, raffle prizes, and a variety of family-friendly activity while the stores are open late. Flushing is known as the Cruise Capital of Michigan and the third Saturday each summer month is great for viewing old time automobiles (all 1972 and earlier).

Riverview Park is the southern starting point of River View Trail. Opened in 2005 and named by the town's residents, River View Trail runs along the north and east side of the meandering Flint River, all the way north to the County Park. Its many lookouts and turnouts each provide you with excellent views of the river. Flushing's Taste of the Trail is an annual August event that gets you going with all sorts of great outdoor activities and a chance to sample the offerings of local restaurants. The Taste of the Trail proceeds goes towards maintenance and expansion of the River View Trail.

In 1835, two years before Michigan became a state, Flushing was founded by brothers Charles and James Seymour. On the Flint River, the Seymours built the area's first sawmill. Flushing, Michigan was named after Flushing, New York which was named after the town of the same name in the Netherlands. Charles had lived in New York's

Flushing and James, an influential state senator, submitted Flushing as the young town's name. In 1837, James suggested that Flushing become the new state's capitol, but his influence had limits.

Flushing was the first small town in Michigan to have electric lights, its power generated from the dam that Oren Hart built across the Flint River. The Hart Dam, long since gone, was at the current location of Riverview Park. The town's 1880 railroad depot is today Flushing's Museum and Cultural Center.

For an interesting, engaging and fun view of Flushing's

history and for just a great read in general, consider "The Situation In Flushing". This book was written in 1965 by Flushing native Edmund Love, who had previously written several best selling books including "Subways Are For Sleeping", the basis of a 1961 Broadway Musical. Love was also a contributor to The Saturday Evening Post, The New Yorker, and Harper's. Love's "The Situation In Flushing" is his account of growing up in Flushing in the early-1900s, but it's also a fascinating look at life all across America at that time. The reader becomes absorbed in the book's characters such as George Love, Edmund's grandfather. Grandpa Love in his youth was a U.P. lumberman who put down his axe long enough to fight the great boxing champion John L. Sullivan to a knockdown, bloody draw. Edmund Love gives you a history lesson disguised as great entertainment.

Additional info about Flushing is available at www. flushingchamber.com.

Area camping: 11 miles west of the Flint River takeout in Montrose is the nearest camping in the area at the Chesaning Show Boat Campground. The campground has 70 wooded sites, both with and without hookups. Their address is 805 South Front Street in Chesaning MI 48616. Call (989) 845-7850 for information or reservations.

THE TAVERN: JACK'S PLACE

Coming in hungry after a day of paddling down the Flint River, it'll make you smile to read at the top of Jack's menu that the sandwiches are "too big to eat alone, too good to share". Bring 'em on! The crack research team's review of the sandwiches, homemade pizza, and burgers were as positive as could be: "perfectly done!" and "excellent!" The specials on barbeque polish hot dogs and NY strips were a great value (or as Jack said, "we're giving them away").

Jack Kern is a very friendly guy, warm and out-going, the perfect personality for a pub owner. This building was originally a used car dealership in the 1950s. When Jack bought the place in the early-70s, it was a big bowling alley separated from a small bar by a wall. Jack took down the wall, making the business more of a tavern than it was.

Table top shuffleboard, which seems to be disappearing from more and more taverns, is a welcome sight. Next to the 5 pool tables are couches, a real comfortable touch. There are also dart boards and big screen TV. All of this is right next to the bowling alley.

Jack's Place has 12 beer tappers going at any one time, with 11 kinds of beer on tap: Bud Light is Jack's number 1 seller and it has two taps, one far left and one far right, to get the wait staff – and the customer - to the most popular brand as quickly as possible.

When Jack bought the bar back in the 70s, drinkers were more discriminating and Pabst Blue Ribbon beer was his best seller. There is still a time at Jack's when Pabst returns to its best selling position, and that's when the live entertainment for the night is the Pole Barn Rebels, also known as the PBRs. Jack said that the very first night the band played at his pub, they had the place jumpin'. His customers noticed that the Pole Barn Rebels were drinking Pabst Blue Ribbon while they were playing (in other words, the PBRs were drinking PBRs) and the crowd dug the music so much, they began to order Pabst, too. That first night of the Rebels playing at Jack's, the customers drank all of the Pabst that Jack had stocked. So, he went to the closest Meijer and bought all of the PBRs that they had. Still not enough. So now, whenever the Pole Barn Rebels are scheduled to play Jack's Place, the bar stocks in heavy quantities of Pabst Blue Ribbon, and once again like in the good old days, Pabst Blue Ribbon beer is #1 at Jack's.

Don't you just love happy endings?

Jack's Place is located at 124 N. Cherry Street in Flushing MI 48433. Phone (810) 659-9881.

Sources: Greg Palinsky, Rebecca Fedewa, Brent LaPonsey, www.flushingchamber.com, www.flushingcity.com, "The Situation In Flushing" by Edmund Love, Jack Kern, Wikipedia

GRAND RIVER
Vandercook Lake MI
Trip 8.7 miles
3 hour & 34 minutes

Canoes & Kayaks supplied by: G.R.E.A.T. Grand River Environmental Action Team, P.O. Box 223, Jackson MI 49204, (517) 416-4234, www.great-mi.org.

Intermediate Ability

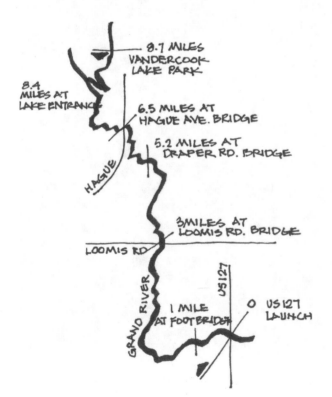

RIVER QUOTES...
- When noted we'd been on the river 1 hour 20 minutes, Maggie replied, "Nay Nay, my shoulder tells me that it's 1 hour 50 minutes, *Shoulder Standard Time*."
- Kenny Price: "I don't have those kinds of problems at my house. I make all of the decisions"; Maggie, "Live alone, do ya?"

THE BACKGROUND: GRAND RIVER

260 miles long, the Grand is the longest river in MI. Its headwaters flow down from their source at Grand Lake, near the town of Liberty (Jackson & Vandercook Lake's neighbor to the south). The Grand River runs north through Jackson and Lansing before turning west to its eventual rendezvous with Lake Michigan. Along its 260 mile journey, the Grand absorbs several tributaries, each over 50 miles long: the Red Cedar in Lansing, the Looking Glass at Portland, the Maple at Muir, the Flat at Lowell, the Thornapple at Ada, and the Rogue at Grand Rapids.

The total Grand River descent, from its headwaters to Lake Michigan, is 552 feet. 400' of that fall takes place before Grand Rapids. Before the first dams were built on the Grand in 1849, there was an 18' descent in a single mile through the town of Grand Rapids. This great whitewater rapids run gave us the fastest one mile stretch of any river in the Lower Peninsula (the Montreal in the U.P. drops 21' per mile).

The earliest white visitors to the river were 1600s Frenchmen. The French christen the river "Grande" reflecting both its length and the size of the river mouth at Grand Haven. They observed 17th century Native American villages on the banks of the Grande in today's Portland, Lyons, Ionia, Lowell, Ada, Grand Rapids, Grandville, (today's ghost town of) Spoonville, and Spring Lake.

The "Grande" was the biggest part of the first recorded crossing of the state by canoe. This statewide adventure took place in 1790. An English explorer and fur trader named Hugh Heward and his group began by traveling northwest from the mouth of the Huron River at Lake Erie in the town now known as Rockwood. Paddling against the current, Heward took the Huron through later day Dexter to Portage Lake. After an 8-mile portage, the group found a tributary that flowed into the Grand River near Jackson. Now canoeing with the current at their backs, Heward and his men paddled the Grand for over 200 miles to its Lake Michigan river mouth at today's Grand Haven. While on the Grand, Heward's party had a bit of a dispute with a band of Indians, resulting in a 50 mile sprint (in one day!) as Heward tried to stay ahead of the feisty Native Americans.

The section of the Grand paddled for this chapter is near the river's headwaters, 20 miles downstream from the river's Grand Lake origins. It earns a degree of difficulty rating of "Intermediate" based on the good steering skills needed for the first third of the trip. This first third stretch takes you down a narrow 'n twisting riverbed with frequent deadwood and leaning trees that you must maneuver around and below.

We paddled the Grand with GREAT, also known as the *Grand River Environmental Action Team.* GREAT is one of the many fine paddling & environmental groups that exist in Michigan. Focused primarily on, but not exclusive to, the Grand River, their paddling trips are fun and their river cleanup efforts are a blessing to anyone who loves Michigan and nature. Their literature states that, "The mission of GREAT is to promote the protection and preservation of the Grand River Watershed through activities and educational programs". The efforts and hundreds of hours invested by GREAT have resulted in, to quote a "Friend of Conservation" award given to them, "a cleaner, healthier, and economically stronger Michigan". We are fortunate to number the members of GREAT among our state's residents. Their website is www. great-mi.org. It is interesting, enlightening, and worth a visit.

The GREAT site lists all of their paddling events, which are open to the public, including maps of put-in and take-out locations. They offer kayaks and canoes at no charge (for your first two times paddling with them) with a reservation made through the email address or phone no.

posted on their website. The fun of GREAT's river trips comes with a big dose of safety: life vests must be worn at all times and they never let a canoe or kayak fall behind the group as GREAT members hang at the back of the flotilla pack, acting as a safety net.

Fish on this section of the Grand include northern pike, bluegill, and largemouth bass.

Crack researchers padding near the Grand's headwaters in late-May were GREAT members including Kenny Price, Kathy Kulchinski, Jon Hoover, Jack Ripstra, Mary Lenardson & Deb Bucholtz along with Vicki Schroeder, Nadia Holyk, Jesse Changa, Dale Kittendorf, Maggie and Doc.

THE RIVER: PADDLING THE GRAND

Launch on US127, 6 miles south of I94 in Jackson. The access is on the east side of 127 across the highway from the Roadside Park. Take out at Vandercook Lake County Park.

Begin by floating beneath US127. Here the river is 25' wide and 2' deep. It quickly narrows to 10' wide. Until reaching the Loomis Road Bridge (3 miles & 1.5 hours in) the river takes you through a tight (10' to 15' wide) and twisty primeval forest with trees leaning in from each river bank and deadwood challenges in the river. Very fun! Past Loomis Road, the river widens and straightens through banks of lowland brush.

.4 mi/11 min: at a left bend is a big tree down, taking up residence across the river for many years to come. Consider passing the tree backwards, utilizing the large turning basin that's before the obstruction, then paddling forward once beyond (allows you to avoid the difficult turn around at the clearance point).

There is a great deal of shade on this section of the Grand as the trees angling in from each shore provide a cooling canopy for the paddling group. Many uprooted trees are showing their bottoms to you, quite risqué.

.9 mi/25 min: for the first time today, you're not floating under a canopy; the river is only partially shaded as there is open farmland on the left.

1 mi/27 min: pass below a footbridge, the trip's 1 mile landmark.

1.4 mi/40 min: at the end of a 150' long straightaway it appears the river is completely blocked by a large logjam; when you are almost upon it, you notice that the river flows through a small opening to the right.

1.8 mi/55 min: a silo is visible in the distance. The Grand is now surrounded by mostly open land.

2.5 mi/1 hr 13 min: the riverbed narrows to 5' wide; there's a rickety old dock along the left shore. 5 minutes downstream a dead creek as wide as the river merges right. There are fields of ferns along both banks.

3 mi/1 hr 26 min: paddle beneath the Loomis Road Bridge.

3.5 mi/1 hr 38 min: at a right river bend a 20' high sandy bank is on the left, the only high bank seen today. The JCC Jackson Community College water tower is soon visible.

4 mi/1 hr 52 min: lily pads cover large sections of the river.

4.5 mi/2 hrs: while paddling a long straightaway, immediately after a small creek merges left, a long & wide channel is on the right. This is the outlet for two lakes, Peter White Lake and Hammer Lake.

4 minutes downstream, a lily pad filled creek enters on a diagonal from the right; one minute later a dead creek as wide as the Grand merges right - do not mistake this for the Grand, and stay left at this junction.

5.2 mi/2 hrs 15 min: you float below the Draper Road Bridge; homes are seen on the right just past the bridge.

The many Orioles perched and flying alongside the group makes one think (for reasons yet unknown) of the old Baltimore Orioles catcher, Andy Etchebarren. In the looks department, Andy was on the same plane as Don Mossi or Leonid Brezhnev.

6.2 mi/2 hrs 37 min: on the right is a dock at the river's edge, leading to a house. 3 minutes downstream, a dock on the left extends over the Grand.

6.5 mi/2 hrs 45 min: paddle under the Hague Avenue Bridge.

7 mi/2 hrs 56 min: from the right, a dead creek 10' wide and thick with obstructions joins the river.

7.3 mi/3 hrs 3 min: to the left, a tiny creek connects the river to a small lake; you're surrounded by reeds along both banks, poking their heads above the water's surface.

8 mi/3 hrs 17 min: from the left, a creek with a straightaway of over 100 yards merges, 20' wide at its mouth. The largest beaver lodge most folks have ever seen is on the left.

8.4 mi/3 hrs 27 min: enter the south end of Vandercook Lake. From here, paddle ahead and to your right, in a NE direction, towards the take-out.

8.7 miles/3 hours 34 minutes: you're in! The access to Vandercook Lake County Park, and to your vehicle, is on the right. The park is located at 4th Street and Avenue A.

THE TOWN: VANDERCOOK LAKE

Detroit Tiger local radio affiliate: WIBM 1450AM

Vandercook Lake, the "Home of the Jayhawks", is a small town on the south side of Jackson. Although this community of less than 5,000 is a very little brother today to Jackson, back in the early-1900s, it was THE place to go, not only for folks from Jackson, but also for those from many miles beyond. Years ago, at the spot where the Grand River paddle ended at Vandercook Lake County Park, was where memories were made.

The Hague Amusement Park was what all of the excitement was about, and was what drew the crowds to Vandercook Lake. From when it opened its doors in the early-1900s until it closed in the 1930s, the Hague Amusement Park was a top of the list destination for families (with their picnic baskets), date nights, kids, and groups. Most arrived on an open air street car, which made a night at the Hague even more exciting.

And what crowds they drew! On holidays, as many as 30,000 gathered for rides like the "Jack Rabbit" rollercoaster and the Ferris Wheel. When the Hague Amusement Park opened at the turn of the last century, it was only a few years since the first Ferris Wheel was introduced to the public at the 1893 Chicago World's Fair. The Ferris Wheel was wildly popular, and a big part of what brought the folks to the park. But as popular as the Ferris Wheel was, the Jack Rabbit rollercoaster was the number 1 attraction, and it was rare that long lines weren't formed to ride it.

Your ticket to the park also allowed you to ride a steamboat on the waters of Vandercook Lake. You could just sit back and tour the lake or dance to the live bands that performed on board. There was also dancing to the music on dry land where nationally known Big Bands could be heard and seen at the park's dance hall. Many folks would cool off during dance hall intermissions by taking a ride on the Jack Rabbit.

The price of admission included a shooting gallery, a roller rink, concession stands, and the very popular picnic area on the edge of the lake. Renting bathing suits and boats were extra.

The park's peak of popularity was from 1910 to 1920. A 1921 fire destroyed the concession area and the roller rink, beginning the park's decline. During the tough times of the Depression, there was no longer money to maintain the park. Buildings, materials, and the rides were gradually sold off. In 1938, the Hague Amusement Park finally closed its doors and became the Vandercook Lake County Park, the Grand River trip's take-out point.

Although the amusement park activities are long gone, today's Vandercook Lake County Park is a great place to go. Located at the intersection of 4th Street and Avenue A, it has a swimming beach, a boat ramp, basketball court, baseball diamonds, picnic shelters, a concession stand, and restrooms.

Area camping:

1. Waterloo Recreation Area, 16 miles northeast of Vandercook Lake. On its 20,000 acres, Waterloo has 4 campgrounds with over 300 sites, cabins, beaches, picnic areas, nature trails, 11 fishing lakes, 47 hiking trails, equestrian trails and the Gerald Eddy Discovery Center. Call 800-447-2757 for information & reservations.

2. Hayes State Park, 12 miles southeast of Vandercook Lake. Located near Brooklyn, Hayes has 185 sites, cabins, picnic area, grills, concession stands, bath houses, and boat launches. Call 517-467-7401 for information & reservations.

THE TAVERN: BONE ISLAND GRILLE

Just one-quarter mile north, a short walk, from Vandercook Lake County Park is a place that draws you back in just like the Hague Amusement Park did a century ago, the Bone Island Grille. The B.I.G. has a Jimmy-Buffett-meets-the-Detroit-Tigers feel about it.

The Bone Island Grille has two halves. The right side is the bar and has Detroit Tiger paraphernalia everywhere. It has a nice belly up to the bar area, multiple big screen TVs to catch the latest Tiger game, and many video games including Ms Pac Man (the classics never grow old). The wall signs are good ones including "Free Beer Tomorrow", giving all of us cause for hope, "If you tap it, they will come", and "Hippies use back door – no exceptions". The best may be the cool neon PBR guitar sign. "The Heathcote Years" at MSU, 1976-1995, are detailed in a great "In Judd We Trust!" poster.

The B.I.G.'s left side is their restaurant and, besides its cool Caribbean Island theme, there is some really good eating over here. Seafood chowder is a customer favorite and what the Bone Island Grille is known for. Also on the menu is the "Buffett Burger", Jimmy B's favorite with lettuce and tomato, Heinz 57 and (of course) French fried potatoes. This was an excellent burger!

To go with the burger, waitress Beth was asked if the B.I.G. carried Pabst Blue Ribbon beer. Yes we do. *In bottles?* No. *Darn.* But we do have it on tap. *Good God Almighty, which way do I steer?*

The Bone Island Grille is located at 4614 Francis Street in Vandercook Lake MI 49203, phone (517) 783-2144.

Sources: Kathy Kulchinski & Kenny Price of GREAT, "The Grand" by Kit Lane, Verlen Kruger Memorial website, Jackson Patriot Citizen

MANISTEE RIVER
Mesick MI
Trip 6 miles
1 hour & 30 minutes

Beginner Ability

Livery: Wilderness Canoe Trips, M37 Bridge (just north of Mesick), Mesick MI 49668, (231) 885-1485, www. wildernesscanoetripsonline.com. Owner Wayne Cotter.

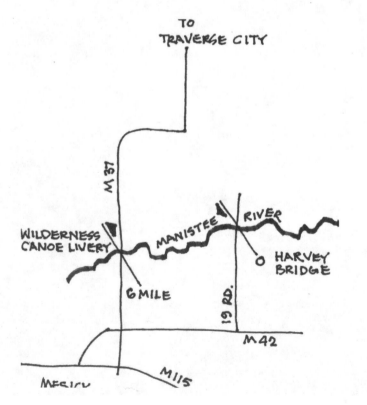

SOUNDTRACK:
Let It Snow – Vaughn Monroe, Good Life – One Republic, Manistee River Waltz – Brian Flechsig & Charlie Weaver, That's All Right – Arthur "Big Boy" Crudup, Brave Sir Robin – Monty Python

RIVER QUOTE...
Kenny: "As soon as you put in, you're in the wilderness"

MILES:
226 mi NW of Detroit, 113 mi North of Grand Rapids, 141 mi SW of Mackinaw City, 266 mi SE of Christmas, 380 mi NE of Milwaukee

THE BACKGROUND: MANISTEE RIVER

At an estimated 198 miles long, the Manistee is one of the longest rivers in Michigan. This state-designated "natural river" has its beginnings northwest of Frederic and Grayling in the DeWard Tract. From there, it meanders southwest through the small towns of Sharon, Smithville (home of the annual Do Ho Row since 1986), and Mesick until it flows into Manistee Lake and then Lake Michigan, in the town of Manistee. The DeWard Tract is a 4,700 acre DNR management area designed as a protective corridor around the tiny stream that is the start of the Manistee River.

The DeWard Tract is named after an area ghost town, DeWard (born 1900/abandoned 1932). DeWard was founded by lumber interests in 1900 specifically to cut down one of the last stands of virgin white pine in Michigan. Arguably the largest sawmill in the entire U.S. was in use in this town until 1912. When the lumbermen were done pillaging the land, the final DeWard resident packed their bags and moved out in 1932.

The headwaters of two of the state's longest and best-known rivers, the Manistee River and the AuSable River, start about 5 miles apart in the middle of the northern Lower Peninsula, a few minutes northwest of Grayling. With the Manistee to the west and the AuSable to the east, they both initially flow straight south for a few miles until turning away from each other at the same latitude as Grayling. From here, the Manistee River streams towards Lake Michigan and the AuSable River towards Lake Huron.

The Manistee River journey outlined in this chapter is near the town of Mesick, 25 miles south of Traverse City. Although beginning in the DeWard Tract as a narrow stream, by the time the Manistee River reaches Mesick (and the lower third of the river's 198 mile journey), it widens to 125'. Through Mesick, the river is gentle-flowing, free of portages and rapids, excellent for family outings and beginners. The speed of the Manistee River during the trip taken for this book was faster than normal because of added water volume from (1) the usual higher water of an early springtime float and (2) 6" of snow falling the night before. The amount of time needed to paddle this section of the river in the summer is 2 hours.

The Manistee has a very peaceful and secluded feel to it, and among the wildlife viewing are deer, wood ducks, beaver, and blue herons. This river year round is a top quality rainbow and brook trout stream. Along with its tributaries, the Manistee River is known among anglers for pike and walleye catches also. Because of its popularity with canoers and kayakers, when this book was published nine canoe/kayak liveries operated along the Manistee to meet the demand for boat rentals.

Crack researchers canoeing and kayaking the Manistee in mid-April were JJ Johnson, Kenny Umphrey and Doc.

THE RIVER: PADDLING THE MANISTEE

Launch several feet upstream from the Harvey Bridge, a short distance northeast of Mesick. On this section of the Manistee, the river width will vary from 60' to 125' and the depth from 2' to holes as deep as 12'.

At the launch, 30' tall banks are to your right, the first of many high ground sightings today. The river immediately has a wonderful wilderness feel to it. Gorgeous tall bluffs and long straight-aways are plentiful on the float.

1 mi/16 min: one mile exactly into this trip, the river bends right around the tip of an oxbow where the land on the left rises to 30' above the water line. There is midstream deadwood to paddle around.

Beaver activity is evident along the shoreline. They've done a fine job of gnawing down trees on the river's edge. From our boats, deer are visible in the nearby woods.

1.4 mi/22 min: at a left river bend is a 70' tall bluff on the right; it's at the end of a long straight-away and especially pretty when first viewed from a distance. On the right, one minute beyond the river bend, steps lead up from the river preceding a merging small creek.

2 mi/30 min: at exactly two miles in, you reach the end of a long straightaway at the base of an 80' tall bluff as the river bends left. We're chasing wood ducks down the river, and they seem none too happy about it.

2.5 mi/36 min: very loud and active, a beautiful little creek merges from the left.

3 mi/43 min: the 2nd of 2 twin creeks is on the left; one minute after the first one merges from the right.

3.3 mi/48 min: preceded by a creek from the left, the land along the left bank looks on its approach like it could be a

golf course (on a snow-covered day, it could be a mirage). A gorgeous bluff sits at the end of a straightaway.

3.6 mi/52 min: as the river gently wraps around to the right, for the first time today and on the left bank you see homes, along with one big dock and stairs.

4 mi/56 min: pass by 2 creeks on the right, the 2nd very loud and pretty, just before the river bends left. View the tallest bluff today, towering 150' above, and upon those heights is the first in a series of homes.

4.5 mi/1 hr 5 min: at a right bend of the Manistee, the creek on the left descends gently down stones to a river rendezvous. It's quite a sight.

4.7 mi/1 hr 7 min: what appears at first glance to be a creek entering the river from your left is actually a split of the river at the upstream end of an island. Staying right at this split gets you to the downstream tip of the island in 3 minutes.

5.4 mi/1 hr 17 min: when you reach the 2-story home with a cinder block lower level on the left, you're within 15 minutes of the trip's end. At the end of a straightaway is a very nice-looking 2-story wooden home with a turret on its right. Fortunately, this turret is decorative and not serving a military function.

You begin to see homes on the elevated left shore. The right bank is low ground.

5.7 mi/1 hr 22 min: there's a little alcove among the homes on the right. Just downstream from the alcove, also on the right, sits a fine looking wood home with an excellent stone chimney.

6 miles/1 hour 30 minutes: you're in! Just a few feet past the M37 Bridge and on the left is the *Wilderness Canoe Trips* livery.

THE TOWN: MESICK

Detroit Tigers local radio affiliate: WMLQ 97.7FM

Mesick, a half-hour drive south on M37 from Traverse City, is known as the Mushroom Capital of the USA. Every Mother's Day weekend since 1959, the town has held their annual Mushroom Festival to celebrate this fact. The festival is one big-time village-wide party. The activities include (of course) a mushroom hunt (mm mm, those morels!), but only after you pick up your Mushroom Picker's Kit, carnival rides (being Mother's Day weekend, Moms ride free), music 'n dancing, flea market, hobby & craft show, carriage rides, horse pull, horseshoe toss, tractor pull, mud bogg (the easy part is driving into the bogg), lucky duck race, parade, variety show, volleyball & softball tournaments, and a beer tent to quench your thirst after the 5K walk/run. There is some good eatin' and a lot of it. To get an idea of how much damage you'll be doing, you can get your blood sugar checked before you start chowing down on barbeque chicken, pasties, baked goods, hot dogs and other festival food.

Almost 100 years before the first Mesick Mushroom Festival, two fur trapping brothers were working their way north along the Manistee River a few miles east of Lake Michigan. In 1864, Howard and Walter Mesick arrived in the vicinity of what is today Mesick, took a liking to the area and decided to do their trapping here. Walter soon left to join the Union Army and fight in the Civil War. Howard stayed to continue trapping. He and his new wife Ellenor obtained a land grant under the Homestead Act good for 160 acres along the Manistee River.

In the mid-1860s, there were quite a few settlers 2 miles north of Howard and Ellenor's farm in the town of Sherman (named after Union General William Tecumseh Sherman). Back in the mid to late 1800s, choosing the location for the railroad to run could make or break a town. Railroad tracks were laid near the sparsely-populated area by Mesick's farm instead of, as expected, through Sherman. Soon, folks from Sherman were trampling back and forth across the Mesick's farm to get to the railroad trains, destroying much of the farm's crops.

To make lemonade from their lemon (in Detroit Tiger speak, to get a Norm Cash for a Steve Demeter), Howard and Ellenor Mesick decided to profit from all of the foot traffic passing over their property by creating a village out of a portion of their farm. The plat of a one square mile village from the Mesick farm was accepted in 1890 by the Michigan state legislature, and the village of Mesick was born.

Howard and Ellenor Mesick did well with their new village, including building the town's 1st store and sawmill. You can learn more about the town of Mesick and its founding couple, as well as about several nearby small towns (including Sherman), at the Mesick Area Historical Museum on 117 Mesick Avenue in Mesick. Ph (231) 946-3958. The Museum website is www.mesickmuseum.com.

Area camping: most of the Manistee River flows through state or federal land, and along the 160 miles of the river serviced by Wilderness Canoe Trips there are 7 different DNR camp sites, each 4-5 paddling hours apart. The sites, all accessible from the river, stretch from minutes west of Grayling to all the way down to Mesick. There is no camping on the Wilderness livery grounds. For information on what each site offers (water? restrooms?) check the livery website or call the livery at (231) 885-1485.

THE TAVERN: BUCKSNORT SALOON

A sign behind the bar reads, "If you're drinking to forget, please pay in advance".

This tavern has been in business quite awhile. When they first opened their doors to the thirsty public, in front of the pub there were horse hitching rails.

You walk in after a chilly day on the river and it's nice to be greeted by a pellet stove fire place, a real nice touch. You can also warm up at the Bucksnort by shooting pool, tossing darts, playing video games, or taking a spin on their dance floor. Nice juke box, too. This would be a fine place to visit in any season.

The burgers didn't last long on our plates. These were very good! The pub has a pizza oven and we heard real good things about the pie from other customers.

There's good value inside these tavern walls. The Bucksnort works hard to stretch your dollar as soon as you walk into the bar. During our visit there was a "Recession Month Special" running: happy hour prices all day, everyday. $1.50 per "mystery shot" is available for the daring. $1 Molsons when a game is on. My Grandfathers, God bless their souls, would've been as happy as I was with $1 Blatz cans all day, everyday. The good value was also on food: from 11-7 daily you get special pricing on the burgers (barely over a buck).

The current owner wasn't around for our visit, but we'd heard a story about the previous owner that makes me smile every time I think about it. He was an old, well-liked, hippie named Dick (may he rest in peace). Seems he kept a shoebox full of bad checks written to the bar. He never went after the check writers, he just kept their bad checks in his shoebox.

The Bucksnort keeps Pabst Blue Ribbon beer longnecks on hand, always a sure sign of quality.

Jim's Bucksnort Saloon is located on M37/M115 at 106 West Mesick Avenue in Mesick MI 49668. Phone (231) 885-2314.

Sources: Wayne Cotter, Michigan DNR, Deborah Kohn & Mesick Historical Society, www.mesick-mushroomfest.org

PAW PAW RIVER
Watervliet MI
Trip 5.7 miles
2 hours & 18 minutes

Intermediate Ability

Livery: Paw Paw River Campground and Canoes, 5355 North M-140, Watervliet MI 49098; (269) 463-5454, www. pawpawrivercampgroundandcanoes.com. Owners Mike and Jeana Gilliam. The livery is two and one-half miles north of I94.

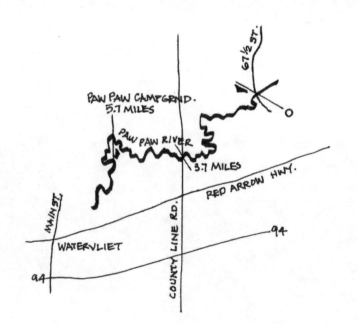

Soundtrack: Scottish Tea – Amboy Dukes, Rising Sun – Sonny Terry and Brownie McGhee, Paw Paw Patch – Perry VerMerris, Fantasie Impromptu Op. 66 (Chopin) – Yundi Li, Ma and Pa Kettle Theme Song

River quote…
Kenny: "Ethan was guiding us down the river"
Ethan: "That might give you a clue why we were hitting so many trees"

Miles: 176 mi West of Detroit, 71 mi SW of Grand Rapids, 308 mi SW of Mackinaw City, 436 mi South of Christmas, 199 mi SE of Milwaukee

Mike and Jeana Gilliam operate two businesses out of the 5355 North M-140 address: their canoe/kayak livery and Ma N Pa's Country Kettle Restaurant & Catering. The star that shines above all else at the restaurant is Jeana's homemade pie menu. Folks have been known to get a whiff of the intoxicating aroma of one of these delights, change their plans for the day, grab a fork 'n hover 'n scarf 'til the last morsel has been savored. Don't think that it can't happen to you 'cause we witnessed the effect that Jeana's pies have on people. The day that we paddled the Paw Paw, a few ladies came in to rent canoes for the afternoon. These gals inhaled the sweet smell from a couple of pies fresh out of the oven,

THE BACKGROUND: PAW PAW RIVER

Pickin' up paw-paws, put 'em in your pockets,
Way down yonder in the paw-paw patch.

Perry serenaded us with this old time kids' song as we paddled down the Paw Paw, but before we talk about the river itself, let's get to the really important stuff: Jeana Gilliam's delicious homemade pies.

into Lake Michigan. Along the way, the Paw Paw River winds its way through the towns of Hartford, Watervliet and Coloma.

The stretch of the Paw Paw detailed in this chapter flows for just over 5 and one-half miles. The fun 2 hour and 20 minute paddle, although through flat water, is challenging. The maneuvering required around deadfall and the trees leaning in from both riverbanks rarely lets up: seldom is there unobstructed paddling of more than a couple of minutes. The river along this trip averages 2' to 3' deep, with the rare 20' deep holes, and a width that averages 30'.

We encountered veteran Paw Paw River canoer Buck Dickie along the way. Buck knows well the entire 66 miles of the river, and says that this is his favorite Paw Paw section.

grabbed forks and ate for a time in a standing position before finally settling into a table and chairs for more pie eating. They never did get out on the water.

The Paw Paw River flows through the extreme southwest corner of Michigan for 66 miles. From its headwaters at the Maple Lake dam in the town of Paw Paw, the river meanders west and then southwest until it merges with the St. Joseph River at Benton Harbor before flowing

There are 40 species of fish in the Paw Paw River including pike, crappies, walleye, smallmouth and rock bass, burbot, and salmon.

Crack researchers paddling the Paw Paw in October, were Kenny Umphrey, Ethan Blake, Cam and Perry VerMerris, and Doc.

THE RIVER: PADDLING THE PAW PAW

Launch from the 67 & ½ Road Bridge, known locally as the Pinery Road Bridge, located to the northeast of Watervliet. Take out at the Paw Paw Campground at Highway M-140 on the north side of town.

.4 mi/10 min: the first merging creek today arrives from your left. The river here runs 2' deep with a hard packed sandy floor.

1 mi/25 min: at 1 mile in, you're paddling on a straightaway through a particularly thick deadwood garden. It's easy to get stuck on the many obstructions below and above the surface.

1.3 mi/33 min: the river bends left and on the right shore is a home with a cinder block lower level. A dry creek bed runs along the downstream side of the home.

1.6 mi/40 min: two creeks roll in from the right as the Paw Paw bends left.

1.9 mi/48 min: at a slight river bend to the left, a very large fallen tree from the right bank allows a short gap along the left shore to pass through.

2 mi/50 min: an excellent picnic landing is found on flat ground on the left shore, just before the river makes a right-hand turn.

2.5 mi/1 hr 4 min: on a straightaway, an island lies left of midstream.

3 mi/1 hr 15 min: just beyond a right bend of the river, a tree leans in from the left bank and lies just above the water line; the most room to limbo beneath the tree is found near the right shore.

3.5 mi/1 hr 26 min: looking down the river, the roof of a home is visible above the tree line beyond the right

bank. Around the next left bend, an uprooted tree on its side on the left bank reaches completely across the river, resting above the waterline as it sits on a right shore tree. There is plenty of paddling space along the right.

3.7 mi/1 hr 30 min: after floating past several homes, you paddle beneath the County Line Road Bridge. As you approach the bridge there is a great deal of deadwood to contend with – stay to the river's center as you travel under the bridge.

A welcoming break spot is on a dirt beach on your left, two minutes downstream from the County Line Road Bridge.

4 mi/1 hr 37 min: a partially-submerged structure is near the right shore; a home is on a bluff as the river bends left.

4.4 mi/1 hr 47 min: lie low in your boat to pass below back-to-back fallen trees. Two minutes downstream, a long creek merges from the right.

4.8 mi/1 hr 55 min: you paddle beneath power lines.

5 mi/2 hrs 2 min: a huge sycamore tree emerges from the river on the right with plenty of paddling room beneath it.

5.2 mi/2 hrs 6 min: a creek merges left as the river bends right.

5.3 mi/2 hrs 8 min: have we paddled into Wisconsin? At the end of a straightaway, as the river bends left, there's a little green and yellow home on the right shore with a Green Bay Packer football helmet painted on the front porch deck's facing.

5.5 mi/2 hrs 12 min: a **_huge_** hallowed out sycamore tree leans into the Paw Paw from the right bank just before the river bends right; from the left, a fine looking and fast moving creek (moving much faster than the Paw Paw itself) winds its way over and around deadwood as it works its way to a merger with the river.

5.7 miles/2 hours 18 minutes: you're in! At the Paw Paw Campground on the right, there's a dirt slope to pull your boat up on.

THE TOWN: WATERVLIET

Detroit Tigers local radio affiliate: WSJM 1400 AM

The town of Watervliet is located deep in the southwest corner of Michigan's Lower Peninsula, 10 miles east of Lake Michigan and 14 miles northeast of Benton Harbor/ St. Joseph. The town and the surrounding area are agriculturally rich, and a leading producer of blueberries, apples, peaches, strawberries, and cherries.

Waterford was the name given to the town when it was first settled in 1833. At that time, a sawmill was built on the Paw Paw River, and the site was given the name of Waterford due to the water flowing through the area. Once it was discovered that another Michigan town already was called Waterford, the village name was changed to "Watervliet", Dutch for "flowing waters".

The spot where the sawmill stood was along the river and on the west side of what is now Highway M-140. That location had served as Watervliet's largest employer for 160 years, first as a sawmill from 1833 to 1893 (for a time it was the largest lumber operation in Van Buren County) and then as a paper mill from 1893 through the mid-1990s.

including Louis Armstrong, Benny Goodman, Jimmy Dorsey, and Lawrence Welk. Doris Day, Perry Como, and Merv Griffin were also among the Crystal Palace Ballroom headliners. Gradually the crowds dwindled and the Ballroom was converted to a roller rink in 1962 before burning down in 1963.

The number of Paw Paw Lake visitors is now fewer than they once were, but the Lake's popularity remains. Smart Money Magazine has called Paw Paw Lake one of the United State's best places in which to buy a vacation home.

Today, driving through the small town of Watervliet (2,000 residents) is a very pleasant surprise. They feature an old-fashioned Main Street, decorated with street lights designed to look like old-time gas lights and antique stores and gift shops to entice the tourists in.

Paw Paw Lake is located just to the north of Watervliet. Its popularity as a tourist hot spot had its peak from the late-1800s to the mid-1900s. As many as 40,000 vacationers would arrive by train each summer, riding double-decked steamboats that would circle the lake, staying & playing at the fifty hotels and the four dance pavilions that lined the eleven mile long shoreline.

In 1925, the biggest Paw Paw Lake dance pavilion of them all was opened, the Crystal Palace Ballroom. The Ballroom, with space for 2,500 dancers, was known as the finest dance hall in all of Michigan. Many of the nationally-known performers from the Big Band Era played here,

Hays Park, along the banks of the Paw Paw River, has a beautiful grassy expanse plus baseball fields, a canoe launch/fishing pier, and a skate park for skate boarders, inline skaters, and BMX bikes. Watervliet is cozy comfortable.

Area camping: right along the Paw Paw River, you'll find plenty of camp space on the canoe livery property. The Paw Paw River Campground and Canoes address is 5355 North M-140, Watervliet MI 49098. Phone Mike and Jeana at (269) 463-5454 for info and reservations. See www.pawpawrivercampgroundandcanoes.com.

THE TAVERN: ELITE BAR & GRILL

When you get a reference for a great post-paddling tavern, and that reference is from a fellow paddler you encounter while out on the river - thank you Buck Dickie - you take it. Buck did not steer (obvious paddling reference) us wrong.

We knew that the Elite Bar & Grill would be good right away. Barely 5' inside the door the twin comments of "I feel really relaxed" and "This place is cool" were uttered.

The Elite, known as E-lite to the regulars, brings in live entertainment for a weekend at a time, then rotates the bands on a once every-four-week schedule. Our hostess Rhonda says the once a month schedule keeps the music fresh. And it's nice to know that you won't have to wait too long to see your favorite band back on the Elite stage.

The hanging green lights throughout the bar are pleasantly hypnotic. Based on the plaques adorning the tavern walls and the 3 pool tables, this is Watervliet's home for pool tournaments, or where folks come to just shoot a few games.

Rhonda told us that for years Elite Bar & Grill used to be right across the street - until the roof caved in (that's one way to broom 'em out at closing time). In 1980, the Elite moved to its present location, an old U.S. Mail building. The current owners have run the place since 2001.

Being simple canoein' folk, we passed on the NY strips and T-Bones offered and went right for the bar burgers. It was a good choice and the result was unanimous: the Elite burgers are excellent! The beer that goes best with a great bar burger just happens to be offered on tap at the E-lite: Pabst Blue Ribbon Beer, always a sure sign of quality.

Although we didn't see any during our tavern visit, the word on the river is that the Elite is where the Paddle Michiana folks come to eat 'n drink after a day on the Paw Paw River. I guess that Great White Bear's like bar burgers, too.

The Elite Bar & Grill is located at 365 S. Main Street (M140) in Watervliet, phone (269) 463-4471.

Sources: Watervliet Paw Paw River Watershed markers, Southwest Michigan Business & Tourism Directory,

PENTWATER RIVER NORTH BRANCH
Pentwater MI
Trip 3.1 miles
1 hour & 20 min.

Livery: Pentwater River Outfitters, 42 West Second Street, Pentwater MI 49449; (231) 869-2999, www.pentwaterriveroutfitters.com. Owner Jeff Jacques.

Beginner Ability

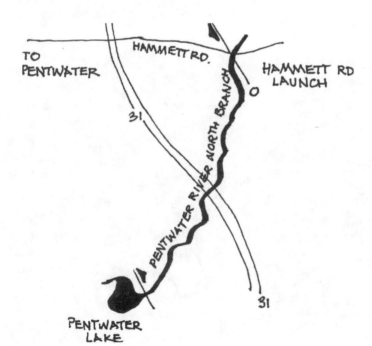

Soundtrack:
Boogie Chillen – John Lee Hooker, Lake of Fire – Meat Puppets, Harbor Lights – Boz Scaggs, 1976 (the Mark Fidrych song) – The Baseball Project, Amoreena (*Dog Day Afternoon* opening sequence) – Elton John

River quote...
Ande the canoeing dog: "This river is grrr-eat!"

Miles:
240 mi NW of Detroit, 84 mi NW of Grand Rapids, 230 mi SW of Mackinaw City, 358 mi S of Christmas, 318 mi NE of Milwaukee WI

THE BACKGROUND: PENTWATER RIVER NORTH BRANCH

The final 3 miles of the Pentwater River North Branch is considered to be the navigable section of the river. Upstream from Hammett Road, the river is too narrow and filled with too many obstructions to provide an enjoyable paddling experince.

Downstream you'll find a different story in a short, sweet & fun beginner-friendly adventure.

This one and one-half hour journey begins at the Hammett Road access, gently meandering generally southward, running parallel to Lake Michigan as it skirts the eastern edge of the town of Pentwater. The North branch flows beneath US31 and Business Route 31 until it empties into the far eastern edge of Pentwater Lake.

During the trip's first hour, the river is narrow and runs a shallow 1' with occasional bottom scraping. The final 20 minutes, near the merger with the South Branch, the river widens as it deepens to between 3' and 4'.

If you'd like to extend the length of the North Branch trip, there is an option: do not exit at the edge of Pentwater Lake. Paddle into the lake and hug its northern (right-hand side) bank for an additional 40 minutes. Keep in mind that there will no longer be a current behind you and that you may encounter headwinds, i.e. this could become a chore or some great exercise depending on your point of view. Take out at the Municipal Boat Ramp by the beach and gazebo on your right.

North Branch wildlife viewing included an eagle soaring in circles high above and a crane surprising us as, out of nowhere, it poked its head above some tall reeds before suddenly taking flight.

Brook, brown and rainbow trout, along with steelhead, run through the river.

Crack researchers paddling the North Branch in late-August were Zachary Stroud, Jane McLaren, Lindsay, Don and (a fine canoeing dog) Ande Rogers, Randy Rea, Cheryl Orgas, Billy and Chris Meeker, Toni LaPorte, Maggie and Doc.

THE RIVER: PADDLING THE PENTWATER NORTH BRANCH

Launch 5 minutes east of downtown Pentwater at the Hammett Road access. Put in 10' upstream from the bridge. The river here is 8' wide and less than 1' deep. Tag alders lean in from both banks.

.3 mi/8 min: "logjam island" passing is easier if you stay left. 2 minutes downstream you float beneath a footbridge. The river is windy, narrow and shallow. The frequent homes seen along the shore do not intrude on the river's tranquility.

1.2 mi/28 min: paddle below the northbound lanes of US31. The river widens to 25' as you skim along the river floor (although never bottoming out).

2 minutes downstream you're beneath the US31 southbound lanes.

2 mi/50 min: paddle under Business Route 31, letting you know that you're exactly two miles into the 3 mile adventure. 30' beyond BR31 and on the right bank is a paved slope leading to a rest area with toilets.

2.1 mi/53 min: 12' wide at its mouth is a creek merging from your left.

2.4 mi/1 hr: enter "cattail gorge" as you paddle among tall cattails along both river banks. These block your view of all else except the sky above.

2.5 mi/1 hr 2 min: the river comes to a "T" as merging from your left, 30' wide at its mouth, is the Pentwater River South Branch. Turn to your right to stay on the North Branch. As a result of the extra volume the South Branch brings to the river, the water depth increases to 4' and it widens to 50'.

3.1 miles/1 hour 20 minutes: you're in! Paddle beneath the Longbridge Road Bridge and enter Pentwater Lake. 20' beyond the bridge, take out on the left bank.

THE TOWN: PENTWATER

Detroit Tiger local radio affiliate: WEFG 97.5FM

A Lake Michigan sunset at the beach (close your eyes and let the mental image sink in for a minute) is just one of the many wonderful moments that the lakefront town of Pentwater offers its guests. Canoeing & kayaking, boating, swimming, fishing, hiking lakeside trails, or visiting the town's many interesting and quaint shops are all lures that bring you back to Pentwater again and again. One of those folks lured back for repeat visits was the creator of the *Peanuts* comic strip, Charles Schultz. The *Peanuts* character Lucy was named and patterned after a member of the family

who owns Pentwater's Safe Harbor Inn (a spirited gal, undoubtedly).

The town's name derived from the formerly "pent" or "penned up" waters of Pentwater Lake. The lake sits just east of Lake Michigan and along the southern edge of downtown Pentwater. In 1855 the lake was penned up no more as in that year Charles Mears had a channel dug. This east-west channel (known as *Mister Mears River*) connected the waters of Pentwater Lake to those of Lake Michigan.

Charles Mears was a lumber baron. He established a sawmill on the north bank of this new channel, a channel he had cut to assist him in moving lumber to his customers in Chicago and elsewhere. Mears business was particularly good in 1871, in the wake of the Great Chicago Fire. Rumors of collusion with Mrs. O'Leary's cow were never proven. His sawmill was working overtime to rebuild Chicago's devastated central business district. That fire was so great that its smoke could be seen in Pentwater, 147 miles away!

From his sawmill on the north bank of the channel, Mears built a pier that stretched 660' out into Lake Michigan. By extending the pier out to where the water is deep, the biggest ships operating on the big lake could pick up cut lumber from the sawmill as well as deliver cargo to Pentwater, aiding the expansion of the young village (established in 1867). In the 1920s, the Mears family donated to the state the land along the channel's north bank, the beginning of what is today Charles Mears State Park.

Charles Mears State Park is one of Pentwater's most popular destinations. The park has plenty of camping space with its 175 sites, and it has a tall wooded dune known as Old Baldy. From various points on Old Baldy, you get an excellent view of the town and of Lake Michigan. You can enjoy their sandy swimming beach and fish from piers adjacent to the park. For more info, go to www.stateparks.com/charles_means.html or call (231) 869-2051.

Pentwater is a wonderful village to visit featuring unique stores, sidewalks with benches and tables, several historical signs, and well-maintained public restrooms. With the area so rich in water, there are several boat launches and marinas in town. If your Pentwater River trip includes an overnight stay, Pentwater offers lodging in beautiful homes, cottages, and bed & breakfasts. See www.pentwatermichigan.com.

Beyond Charles Mears State Park, camping at Pentwater is available at River Farm Campground on 5480 N Wayne Rd (231) 869-8127 and Whispering Surf on 7070 South Lakeshore Drive (231) 869-5050.

THE TAVERN: THE BROWN BEAR

This fine village pub hangs its hat on burgers. They advertise themselves as the "Home of the notorious Bear Burger". A sign inside reads, "Thanks for helping make the Brown Bear West Michigan's #1 burger joint". Several of our crack research team members had a Brown Bear burger, and the sounds of "mm mm!" were unanimous.

The bar burgers come in 3 sizes: the quarter pound "Wimpy", and half pound "Cub" and the one pound "Bear". Toni was plenty satisfied after her quarter-pounder, saying that "The Wimpy is not so wimpy". After these burgers, all traces of hunger had disappeared from our table of paddlers.

All traces of thirst were soon gone also. The thirst was in part knocked down by Henry Weinhard's brand root beer. Billy gave this the highest praise possible, commenting that it tastes as good as top-notch classic root beers Hires and Dad's. Our thirst was also attended to by the longnecks of Pabst Blue

Ribbon beer, always a sure sign of quality.

The Brown Bear is not as old as many of the bars written about in this book, but it has the comfortable feel of one that has been around for awhile. Inside it is tongue-in-groove pine with a cedar back bar. Downstairs is where the main bar is along with a pool table and many great sports photos including one of the Olympia, hallowed ground of the Detroit Red Wings, and another displaying early arenas of hockey's Original 6 teams. Regarding the quality of the bar's juke box, when John Lee Hooker's "Boogie Chillen" is the first song that you see, well, that's a good sign.

Upstairs features its own bar. Among its excellent photos is one of the Rat Pack shooting pool and workers in 1932 at the Rockefeller Center, legs dangling from scaffolding high above NYC. Beyond the indoor seating up here, there are 6 tables on an outdoor balcony, perfect for drinking, dining, and people watching on the street below.

Velinda was both our waitress and bar historian. She is very good at both of these jobs. Velinda told us that Andy Carter owns two Brown Bear pubs, this one in Pentwater and one in Shelby. Originally, this building housed a movie theatre. It was then transformed into a succession of taverns including the *Wheel In*, then the *Belly-Up*, and finally in 2003 it was renamed The Brown Bear. A 2006 remodel turned the upstairs from an office and storage space into the fine spot that it is today.

Oh yeah, don't forget to order the onion rings.

The Brown Bear is located at 278 N Hancock Street in Pentwater, (231) 869-5444.

Sources: Pentwater Historical Society, Pentwater Chamber of Commerce, Charles Mears State Park, www.safeharborinn. com. Velinda at the Brown Bear

PIGEON RIVER
Grand Haven MI
Trip 3.8 miles
1 hour & 45 minutes

Beginner Ability

Livery: Lakeshore Kayak Rental, 14023 Green Street (in Felix's Marina), Grand Haven MI 49417; (616) 566-1325, www. lakeshorekayakrental.com. Owners - Karen and Bob Chapel. Lakeshore also services the Grand River and Crockery Creek.

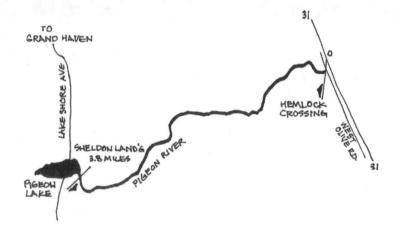

SOUNDTRACK: My Uncle Used to Love Me but She Died – Roger Miller, Rockin' Robin – Bobby Day, How Long – David "Honeyboy" Edwards, Mister Blue Skies – ELO, Ramblin' Rose – MC5

RIVER QUOTE...
Kenny (on Aubrey's snacking): "Not one Dorito was lost in the paddling of this river"

MILES: 192 mi West of Detroit, 34 mi West of Grand Rapids, 263 mi SW of Mackinaw City, 391 mi South of Christmas, 263 mi East of Milwaukee

THE BACKGROUND: PIGEON RIVER

The Pigeon River, also known as Pigeon Creek, winds to the west midway between Grand Haven to its north and Holland to its south. It is a little 9 mile long river that comes to an end as it flows into Pigeon Lake, which in turn empties into Lake Michigan.

Launching at Hemlock Crossing, the final 3.8 miles of the Pigeon River is the segment of the river outlined in this chapter. It is considered to be the navigable section of the river, as upstream from Hemlock it is too narrow and too clogged with deadwood to allow for a fun day on the water.

These 3.8 miles create a very leisurely paddle, even in high water, fast flowing spring conditions. Keep in mind that the one hour and 45 minutes required to float the Pigeon River in April for this chapter's trip would be a quicker time than in "normal" summer time conditions (likely a 2 hour 15 minute summer trip). There are obstructions to steer your way through, but they are few. The Pigeon is scenic, charming, and accessible to canoers & kayakers of any skill level.

The Hemlock Crossing Nature Center offers an excellent canoe and kayak launch. In addition, its 239 acres of woods and wetlands have 6 miles of hiking and cross country ski trails that take you through forests and old pine plantations. Hemlock has several scenic river overlooks, two picnic shelters, and an informative (and fine looking) nature education center.

To get to the Hemlock Crossing launch site: Take US31 to Croswell Street, midway between Grand Haven and Holland. Travel west (towards Lake Michigan) on Croswell and in just a few feet you're at West Olive Road. Turn left (south) on to West Olive. In 3/10ths of a mile, Hemlock Crossing will be on your right at 8115 West Olive Road in West Olive MI 49460, phone (616) 786-4847.

To get to the Port Sheldon Landing (also known as Sheldon Landing Township Park) take out access: Take US31 to Croswell Street and travel west (towards Lake Michigan). Take Croswell to Lakeshore Drive and turn left (south). In 1 mile the Port Sheldon site will be on your left, just before crossing over Pigeon River.

Sharing the Pigeon with you will be brown trout, bass, pike, and sunfish.

Crack researchers paddling the Pigeon River on April 30 were Kenny, Brian & Aubrey Umphrey, Mister P Pienta, and Doc.

THE RIVER: PADDLING THE PIGEON

Launch at the Hemlock Crossing kayak/canoe landing. The river width will increase from 15' the first 1.5 miles to as wide as 70' after the 2 mile mark. The river depth averages 3'.

.2 mi/5 min: paddle beneath a very nice footbridge, part of the Hemlock Crossing walking trail. In the early going, the narrow riverbed winds through tight turns.

.4 mi/8 min: the Hemlock Crossing Nature Center is visible on the left. You're floating through long, winding S-curves. It is absolutely beautiful out here with lowlands nearby and gorgeous tall trees in the distance.

.6 mi/15 min: as the river makes a hard right, a park observation deck is directly above the river on the left shore.

1 mi/27 min: after the river bends right, at the end of a long straightaway inconspicuous power lines barely are visible. With the strong winds, Mister P notes that "those pine trees are swaying to the music".

1.4 mi/37 min: on the left, see the first two homes on this stretch of the river.

1.5 mi/40 min: a very large fallen tree allows passing on the extreme right; approach slowly while hugging the right bank. It took our crack research team 5 minutes to work our way through the obstruction. The river widens to 30'.

1.7 mi/51 min: a log cabin is on the left shore. Turtles and magnificent pine trees are everywhere.

2.3 mi/1 hr 8 min: pretty little creek merges right near a beaver dam; there are long stretches of cattails and water lilies along the left bank.

2.6 mi/1 hr 16 min: you're beneath the power lines. On the left shore is a "river access private" sign. There are many large, attractive riverside homes. This is where the money flows.

2.8 mi/1 hr 24 min: a creek enters the river on your right. Directly across the river beyond a wide expanse of flat land is a very, very large home. 3 minutes downstream, a creek merges from the left.

3.1 mi/1 hr 30 min: a golf course is on the left and its huge clubhouse is in the distance. The flat stone embankment is by the 11th hole.

2 mi/58 min: on the left bank, if you're paddling the Pigeon during late-April/early-May, the forsythia bush in front of a home with a brick chimney will be a spectacular yellow.

2 minutes downstream, come upon a big island. Pass either left or right during times of high water, but it's only 6" deep on the left even in elevated spring time river levels. It will take 7 minutes to reach the downstream tip of the island.

2.1 mi/1 hr 4 min: on the left shore is a unique home with windows from floor to ceiling, two stories high with 5 peaks.

2.2 mi/1 hr 7 min: a big right bank hill below is below the power lines. The river widens to 70'.

3.7 mi/1 hr 42 min: by homes on the left, a dirt road leads to the shoreline at the footings of what once was the Holly Drive Bridge.

3.8 miles/1 hour 45 minutes: you're in! Take out on the right shore at the Port Sheldon Landing. Visible ahead is the Lakeshore Drive Bridge. Beneath the bridge is where the Pigeon River empties into Pigeon Lake. Standing on the bridge, you can see Lake Michigan beyond Pigeon Lake.

THE TOWN: GRAND HAVEN

Detroit Tigers local radio affiliate:
WBBL 107.3FM

Among the 187 U.S. Metro areas that *Gallup and Healthways* surveyed in 2010, Grand Haven-Holland was ranked #1 in the nation on their "basic needs/safety index" and #2 on the "well being/happiness index". So the entire country knows now what Michigan residents have known for years: Grand Haven is wonderful. Since it is the only city, town or village in the world that is named Grand Haven, that makes it uniquely wonderful.

The one of a kind name was given to the town in 1835 by the man who platted it, Rix Robinson. Rix thought that since the town's port was so large (Grand), at the river mouth of the Grand River, and its harbor safe (Haven), that *Grand Haven* was the perfect name.

The town was almost named Stuart by its 1834 founder, the Reverend William Ferry (the same man who laid out the village plans for Montague), after the reverend's friend, Robert Stuart. The town that sits beautifully in its wooded dunes and is surrounded by the waters of Lake Michigan, Spring Lake, and the Grand River deserves the name Grand Haven.

William Ferry was not only Grand Haven's founder, but also its first postmaster (1835-1853). The first recorded instance of postal service in west Michigan was in 1835 when Native Americans carried mail from Grand Rapids to Grand Haven.

One hundred and fifty-foot tall white pine trees were once found for miles around Grand Haven. The dense pine forest was irresistible to lumber interests who descended upon the area as early as 1836. The towering white pines were cut to provide lumber for Chicago, Milwaukee, and many other port cities.

In 1871, at the corner of Washington and Third Streets, Mister W.C. Sheldon opened his Magnetic Mineral Springs, to cure what ails you. W.C. Sheldon's popular corner store is considered to represent the birth of tourism in Grand

Haven. The town's tourism industry is alive and well today. People from Michigan and all over the Midwest are drawn to Grand Haven for the gorgeous sandy beaches of Lake Michigan, the fabulous Chinook salmon fishing in the Big Lake, the entertaining Musical Fountain (the world's largest when it was built in 1963), its dunes, the pier and lighthouse, quaint downtown shops, and the striking views which seem to be everywhere (including those marvelous Lake Michigan sunsets).

Not all of the town's gifts are along or in the water or downtown. Grand Haven's Central Park is a splendid place to visit. The park covers an entire city block, with Columbus to the north, Washington to the south, 4th Street to the west, and 5th Street to the east. Here you can find the land-based peacefulness that you'd find out on the river. In the exact center of this superb green expanse is a large fountain. There is a monument to those who fought in World War I. You'll find park benches, works of art, and gardens. Central Park is definitely worth a visit.

There are so many festivals, events, fun things to do, inns, lodges, and B&Bs that they cannot all be listed here. For a complete and great source of info on Grand Haven go to www.visitgrandhaven.com.

Stuart, Michigan? No, *Grand Haven* is exactly what it should be known as. Thank you Rix Robinson.

Area camping: Grand Haven State Park is a 48-acre park with a wonderful sandy beach on the shores of Lake Michigan. GHSP has 174 campsites, great swimming in the Big Lake, a picnic area, and playground. At the park is the Grand Haven Lighthouse. Taking a walk on the pier to the lighthouse is an annual event for many families. The park is on the south side of Grand Haven at 1001 Harbor Avenue. Phone (616) 847-1309.

THE TAVERN: SNUG HARBOR

Location, location, location: there are few better than the outdoor deck at Snug Harbor, right on the waterfront and just south of downtown Grand Haven. Sitting on their deck, you have a fabulous elevated view of the last few hundred feet of the 260-mile long Grand River. What a glorious sight, watching the state's longest river as it flows by Grand Haven's pier and lighthouse and then empties into Lake Michigan. Viewing boats traversing the Grand, going to and from the lake at sunset, creates a pretty spectacular memory.

Snug Harbor's outdoor deck seats 80 and is the blue collar brother to the upscale Jelly's, located indoors and right next door. The deck has a great wind-in-your-hair, sand-in-your-shoes, party feel to it. It features a well-stocked bar and their burgers, well, adding condiments would be a waste because these are excellent!

Relaxing on the deck at Snug Harbor is the perfect end to a perfect day on the Pigeon.

Snug Harbor is located at 311 South Harbor in Grand Haven, phone (616) 846-8400. Their website is www.harborrestaurants.com/snugharbor

Sources: Karen and Bob Chapel, Sue and Kristen Hintz at Hemlock Crossing, Grand Haven Chamber of Commerce, Tri-Cities Historical Museum, Dan O'Keefe, Dr. Neil MacDonald

PRAIRIE RIVER
Centreville MI
Trip 5.4 miles
2 hours & 5 minutes

Livery: Liquid Therapy Canoe & Kayak Rentals, 221 S. Main Street, Three Rivers MI 49093; (269) 273-9000, www. liquidtherapypaddling.com. Owners Ernie Manges and Karen McDonald

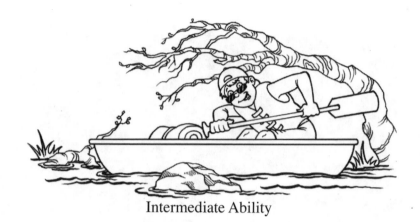

Intermediate Ability

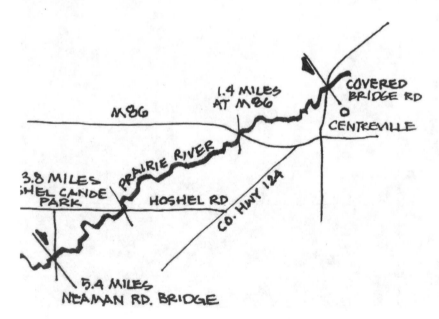

SOUNDTRACK: Left Over Biscuits - Schlitz Creek, Prairie Rose – Roxy Music, Cold Cuts – Albert Collins, One Dime Blues – Etta Baker, Footprints In The Snow – Rem Wall and the Green Valley Boys

RIVER QUOTES...
- Tommy to Liquid Therapy owner Ernie: "Ernie, you gotta clear that river wood for us" Ernie to Tommy: "This ain't no Disneyland ride."
- Tommy: "Hey Kenny, how's Wilbur (Kenny's pet donkey) doing?
Kenny: "Hee Haw right."

MILES: 163 mi SW of Detroit, 78 mi South of Grand Rapids, 318 mi SW of Mackinaw City, 436 SE of Christmas, 230 mi SE of Milwaukee

THE BACKGROUND: PRAIRIE RIVER

The Prairie River flows for 50 miles through the southwest corner of Michigan's Lower Peninsula. Its run begins about 12 miles southeast of the town of Nottawa. From there it flows through Prairie River Lake, meandering west through the towns of Nottawa and Centreville, until it empties into the St. Joseph River a few minutes south of the town of Three Rivers.

The section of the Prairie River detailed in this chapter is a 5 mile run. The 2 hour paddle is through a moderate 2.5 mph flat water current that begins on the north side of Centreville and ends a couple of hours before it merges with the mighty St. Joseph River. You're treated to a fun challenge as you maneuver under and around the frequent fallen deadwood and leaning trees. The river floor is sandy throughout. The ground is so low on both riverbanks that, in the spring or other high water times, trees among the deep woods on the shorelines would be standing in the river, giving the Prairie a real bayou look.

Apart from the wonderful Canoe Island at the 90 minute mark, good riverbank break spots are few. The water depth ranges from 1' to 4' and the river width from 25' to 50'.

The crack researchers paddling the Prairie River in October were Kenny Umphrey, Ethan Blake, Tommy Holbrook, and Doc.

THE RIVER: PADDLING THE PRAIRIE

Launch from the Covered Bridge Road one mile north of M86 in Centreville. There's a fine access park on the south bank of the Prairie and on the west side of the road. Take out at the Neaman Road Bridge.

There's action right out of the starting gate. Within the first 5 minutes of this stretch of the Prairie, there are four separate paddling challenges, forcing you to make quick decisions as you wind around deadwood and limbo under trees through tight turns in the river. Very exciting!

.9 mi/23 min: after seeing three large trees ripped from the ground and lying on their sides, a long creek emerges from your right. Blue Herons are sighted.

1 mi/27 min: you'll know that you're 1 mile in when the river bends left and a cornfield sits at the top of a high right bluff. Encounters with fallen trees decrease and there's more open water.

1.4 mi/36 min: just before paddling beneath the M86 Bridge, the large structure on the right is the St. Joseph County Road Commission building. Downstream from the bridge, the river widens to 50' on the calm straightaway.

1.7 mi/42 min: at a left bend, the river narrows and multiple deadwood obstructions lie ahead to maneuver through.

1.9 mi/48 min: the ruins of an old dock are on the right.

2.5 mi/1 hr: the river narrows as it wraps around a left bend; a little lagoon lies to the right; there's a small, grassy island near the left bank. A weathered wooden shelter on the right shore is fronted by a small dock.

2.9 mi/1 hr 10 min: float below the Strobel Road Bridge and its old wooden cross beams. One minute downstream you're among a series of small islands and below two sets of power lines.

3.5 mi/1 hr 22 min: a large creek merges from the left near a midstream island at a river right bend. Urban landscaping is displayed on the left bank.

3.7 mi/1 hr 26 min: reach the upstream edge of a big island. It's suggested that you follow the main flow left around the island as there are obstructions to the right.

3.8 mi/1 hr 28 min: the beautiful island on your right, just before the Hoshel Road Bridge, is the *Hoshel Canoe Park*. This excellent break spot provides you with picnic tables, a grill, and trash cans. Based on the number of trees on the island, there are 9 restrooms. A small footbridge connects Hoshel Canoe Park to Hoshel Road.

4.1 mi/1 hr 38 min: two homes on the right bank precede an island downstream.

4.5 mi/1 hr 46 min: as the river bends left, there's a willow tree along the right bank and a farm beyond the right shore.

5 mi/1 hr 57 min: you wind through a series of leaning and fallen trees.

5.1 mi/1 hr 59 min: two trees fallen from the right shore allow a small gap to paddle through on the far left.

5.2 mi/2 hrs: pass by the beautiful cedar home on the left before paddling through a whitewater run.

5.4 miles/2 hours 5 minutes: you're in! Take out on the right just before the Neaman Road Bridge.

THE TOWN: CENTREVILLE

Detroit Tigers local radio affiliate: WMSH 1230 AM

As M86 takes you to the edge of town, the sign reads, "Welcome to Centreville, Hometown of actor Verne Troyer, Graduate of Centreville High School 1987". Outside of Centreville, Verne is best known as Mini-Me in the Austin Powers movies. The nearby community college that Verne attended installed a special lowered door handle for him on one of his classroom doors.

Centreville is 35 minutes south of Kalamazoo and gets its name from its location at the exact center of St. Joseph County. The village was settled in 1831 and is the county seat. In the center of the town square is their Victorian-style courthouse, its full name the St. Joseph County Courthouse, built in 1899 and dedicated in 1900. The red brick and sandstone courthouse features marble floors, frosted glass doors, and beautifully-carved woodwork, all constructed at a cost of $33,000.

The town's first settler, Thomas W. Langley, was a thirsty soul. He arrived in town in 1831 and promptly built a tavern. To show their thanks, the town folk in 1887 erected a bridge in his honor, which can still be seen today. The Langley Covered Bridge is the oldest standing wooden covered bridge in Michigan. You can see the still active bridge by taking Covered Bridge Road /County Road 133 for 3 miles north of Centreville (two miles north of the Prairie River).

Held every year since 1851 in Centreville's Fairgrounds is the *St. Joseph County Grange Fair* (also known as the Centreville Fair), with festivities beginning on the 3rd Sunday in September. When the Michigan State Fair was suspended in 2010 (after running from 1849 to 2009), Centreville's Fair became the oldest running fair in the country.

In the fair's early days, as the 1800s became the 1900s, fairgoers could take balloon rides (known as "balloon ascensions"), watch men assemble and then fly airplanes, and take in a baseball game.

The St. Joseph County Grange Fair is annually ranked among the top 5 in Michigan. Fair visitors are treated to carnival rides, midway games, live music (hello George Jones!), a rodeo, horse shows, harness racing, tractor pulls, and a demolition derby. 150,000 people each year attend the fair's fun (the entire St Joseph County population is only 62,000). For more information about the fair, go to www.centrevillefair.com.

THE TAVERN: THE ROUND UP

The Round Up has been in business long enough that Rem Wall, the old time country singer, used to play here. More about that in a bit…

This is a tavern that's real comfortable, laid-back, and welcoming to out-of-towners. The Round Up is as old as the town itself, where everyone knows everyone, and where Centreville gathers to meet.

Just like life outside the tavern's doors, this place is owned and run by women. Linda Mullins and her daughter Kim Hilman take care of the men who belly up to the bar, men who belly up _early_ to the bar, sometimes waiting outside for the tavern doors to open at 11AM. These regulars star once a year, every November, in the "last chance prom". This is a prom for adults, where the men dress up like "Miss Americas", a very scary America.

The Round Up is known for its burgers, but the chili

dog that Stacey brought to the table hit the spot. The tavern's location across the street from the historic St. Joseph County Courthouse makes this a favorite lunch spot for the courthouse employees. In recognition of the Round Up's neighbor, the tavern serves up a half-pound of good eatin' with their Court House Hamburger.

Before there was Hank, there was Rem Wall. Beginning in the 1940s, you could find Rem and his Green Valley Boys occasionally playing a set at the Round Up. Based out of Kalamazoo, Rem and the boys performed, it was said, "a mighty fine brand of hillbilly music". For 30 years of Saturday nights, from 1950 to 1980, Rem Wall and the Green Valley Boys starred on the weekly barn dance, "the Green Valley Jamboree", broadcast on Kalamazoo's WKZO to over 4 million weekly radio listeners and, later, TV viewers in Michigan and Indiana. Rem's fans stretched far beyond the Midwest: the former West German Chancellor, Willy Brandt, was a self-proclaimed big Rem Wall fan.

Willy Brandt would've been right at home bellied up to the bar with the 11AM Round Up regulars, washing down his half-pound Court House burger with a fine German beer like Pabst Blue Ribbon. *We'd like to teach the world to swig, in perfect harmony...*

The Round Up is located at 116 E. Main Street (M86) in Centreville, phone (269) 467-6085.

Sources: Info MI, www.examiner.com, www.centrevillemi. com, Michigan Historic Site markers, www.visioncouncil.org, Round Up's Linda Mullins & Stacey

RED CEDAR RIVER
East Lansing MI
Trip 10.6 miles
3 hours & 15 minutes

Intermediate Ability

Livery: MSU Bikes on Michigan State's campus, B10 Bessey Hall, East Lansing MI 48824, (517) 432-3400, http://bikes.msu.edu

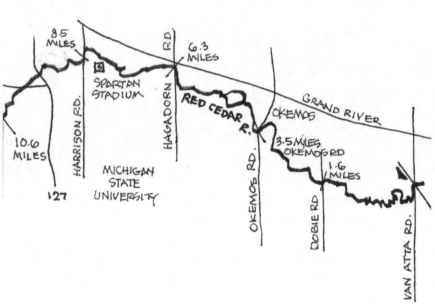

RIVER QUOTE...
Dana about her spill "It was a soft tip, kind of like... *I... guess... I'm... going... in*"

MILES: 92 mi NW of Detroit, 72 mi W of Grand Rapids, 228 mi S of Mackinaw City, 356 mi SE of Christmas, 312 mi East of Milwaukee WI

THE BACKGROUND: RED CEDAR RIVER

The Red Cedar River flows for 45 miles, cascading down from its headwaters at Cedar Lake, south of Fowlerville. The river meanders through Williamston, Okemos, East Lansing and then Lansing before it empties into the Grand River.

This chapter's Red Cedar River journey takes you through the heart of the Michigan State University campus. In the mid-1800s, with the population of the campus and the town then known as "Collegeville" barely numbering in the hundreds, the thought of students scattered along the riverbanks, studying and writing papers, creates an idyllic river image.

Pollution of the Red Cedar is a problem that has existed at least since the first year East Lansing became a city: in 1907 it was determined that the answer to the town's needs for drainage (stagnant water was prevalent) and sewers was to dig a tunnel to carry raw sewage and excess water into the Red Cedar near where today runs the intersection of Harrison Road and Michigan Ave. As a result, by the 1920s the untreated sewage pouring into the Red Cedar had become a major health problem.

The fortunes of the river took a positive turn in the 1970s when major improvements in East Lansing's sewage treatment plant occurred with

a stated goal to clean up the Red Cedar River. The improved health of the Red Cedar is reflected in its increased fish population, including growing numbers of smallmouth bass, smelt, and steelhead.

Among the individuals & groups contributing to this good news are the Michigan State University Institute of Water Research and MSU Landscape Services, who've created riverside vegetative buffers that filter out pollutants from the Red Cedar. These buffers also serve to absorb water from heavy rains, to minimize overwhelming the river with huge water surges. Volunteers assist with river cleanups including those sponsored by the MSU Fisheries and Wildlife Club, among others.

The river earns a degree of difficulty ranking of "Intermediate" due to (1) frequent obstructions that must be paddled around and (2) rapids near the MSU Administration Building. Keep in mind that the times recorded were from a spring trip and four days after a 3" rainfall, so that water levels were higher and currents faster than normal.

There was great wildlife viewing in and along the Red Cedar. Muskrat, deer and geese were spotted on this trip.

Crack researchers on the Red Cedar in May were the *Go Green, Go White, Go Paddling* team of Debbie Theodoroff, Jim "JJ" Johnson, John Newman, Paul Forsberg, Dana and Jimmy Gretzinger, and Doc.

THE RIVER: PADDLING THE RED CEDAR

Launch just east of Okemos in Legg Park at Van Atta Road, directly to the right of the parking lot, and take out at the Aurelius Road Bridge in Lansing.

Within the first three-tenths of mile, four logjams are encountered that, in this high water, are challenging but possible to paddle over or around. There's a very bayou-feel to the area, with standing and leaning trees both on the shore and in the water. A thick canopy of trees is overhead.

.3 mi/11 min: a nice looking creek merges with speed from the right.

.6 mi/16 min: "Natural Area" sign sits on the left bank.

.9 mi/22 min: on a little bluff on the left is the first house seen on this stretch of the river. More left bank homes will follow.

1.6 mi/37 min: float beneath the Dobie Road Bridge.

1.9 mi/43 min: across from each other on both riverbanks are the original concrete footings of "old" Dobie Road.

2.3 mi/50 min: rolling down the 10' bluff on the left is a small stream. The Red Cedar is 30' wide here and continues to be over-the-paddle deep. Homes begin to appear along the right shore, soon to be seen beyond both riverbanks.

3.2 mi/1 hr 5 min: on the right shore, a nice little wooden deck sticks out over the river, just a few steps down from its home.

3.5 mi/1 hr 10 min: on the left shore is a park with restrooms. 2 minutes past the park, the river flows below the Okemos Road Bridge. Just past the bridge, the Red Cedar narrows to 25' wide.

4.6 mi/1 hr 27 min: paddle beneath the Nakoma Drive Bridge. Grand River Avenue is unseen from the water, but only 200' to your right. On the left shore, both before and after the bridge, is the Indian Hills Golf Course.

5 mi/1 hr 33 min: there is a very large pond, almost a small lake, on the right, while the river flows left.

5.3 mi/1 hr 38 min: there is a major obstruction in the middle of the river and a very fun rapids flowing around it both right and left.

5.5 mi/1 hr 43 min: pass below a railroad bridge. This precedes a beautiful canopy of trees over the river.

6.3 mi/1 hr 58 min: you're paddling beneath the Hagadorn Road Bridge, entering the Michigan State University campus property.

6.8 mi/2 hrs 7 min: passing under Bogue Road Bridge. Red Cedar trees are downstream on the right shore, near the Kresge Art Center.

7.2 mi/2 hrs 12 min: paddle beneath Farm Lane Road Bridge. Just beyond the bridge and on the right shore is the Red Cedar River canoe livery, MSU Bikes.

7.4/2 hrs 16 min: float below a pedestrian bridge. Rapids are downstream from here. They cannot yet be seen, but they can definitely be heard. You'll be into these rapids in just one-tenth of a mile.

The Red Cedar River Rapids...

These rapids are brief, but can be vicious. The GPS recorded a rapids speed of 9 mph. There's a big drop as soon as you enter, and a rocky trip once you hit the bottom of that drop. The first clue that the rapids may be difficult to navigate safely: as you approach the rapids, several dozen students on the river banks flipped out their cell phones to record death photos.

Two of our canoes ran these and both were successful, but it is strongly suggested that you pull over to the left shore (the best place for a portage) to scout the rapids before deciding to run them. In the late-summer, there is often insufficient water levels to paddle through the rapids.

A pedestrian bridge crosses the river just downstream from the rapids.

7.6 mi/2 hrs 20 min: beyond the left shore, Spartan Stadium is visible through the trees. On the right shore is the campus Main Library.

7.7 mi/2 hrs 25 min: float beneath the bridge at IM Sports Circle. The Sparty Statue is not visible from the Red Cedar River and it is just beyond the left shore.

8.3 mi/2 hrs 35 min: paddle alongside the Kellogg Center on the right and float under a pedestrian walkway. Jenison Field House is to the left. A second pedestrian walkway is the main connector between the Kellogg Center and Spartan Stadium.

8.5 mi/2 hrs 39 min: the river flows below the Harrison Road Bridge. The Breslin Center is in the distance to your left.

8.9 mi/2 hrs 45 min: the 9-hole Red Cedar Municipal Golf Course is on the right.

9 mi/2 hrs 48 min: trees are leaning low across the water for several bends, creating a fun paddling challenge.

9.2 mi/2 hrs 51 min: paddle beneath the Kalamazoo Road Bridge. Dagwood's Tavern is 1/4 mile to your right. The Lansing Riverwalk, also known as the Lansing River Trail, is along the right bank. It runs a total of 8 miles along the Red Cedar and Grand Rivers.

9.5 mi/2 hrs 55 min: float below US127.

9.8 mi/3 hours: float below I496. In two minutes, you paddle below a rail bridge.

10.1 mi/3 hrs 4 min: the Riverwalk crosses the river, taking walkers into nearby scenic wetlands and woodlands.

10.4 mi/3 hrs 10 min: pass below another rail bridge.

10.6 mi/3 hrs 15 min: you're in! Just before the Aurelius Road Bridge, take out on the left shore at the *Ralph W. Crego Park - Kruger's Landing – City of Lansing* ramp.

THE TOWN: EAST LANSING

Detroit Tiger local radio affiliate: WVFN 730AM

1907 was the year when East Lansing was incorporated as a city. However, the actual commencement of the college town took place a half-century before…
"The campus of the college was only a clearing in the great Michigan forest" was the observation of a local resident when the college that would become Michigan State University was born in 1855. The ten homes of the Agricultural College's "Faculty Row" made up the beginning of the East Lansing community.

It was along the Red Cedar's riverbanks in 1855 that the Michigan legislature established a college for teaching scientific agriculture. To quote John C. Holmes, one of the major organizers of the college, the goal was "to create a school that would make scientists of Michigan's largest occupational group: the farmer". The post office of the day received mail addressed to "Agricultural College, Michigan". Graduates would apply what they learned to their home farms, neighbors would watch and learn, the wisdom would radiate out and improved production would be widespread. The college did not seek to educate every farmer, but it did seek to train leaders. From its earliest days, the new school's curriculum included math, history, philosophy, English, physics, chemistry and botany.

In 1862, President Abraham Lincoln signed into law the Morrill Act. Also known as the "Land Grant" Act, this rewarded colleges that taught agriculture, engineering & military tactics "to educate the industrial classes in the several pursuits and professions in life" (i.e. so that the working class could obtain a practical education). The State Agricultural College, what Michigan State U. was known as in 1862, was the prototype college for this act. Their initial reward was a federal government land grant of a quarter million acres in the northern Lower Peninsula (eventually sold off by MSU to create a $1M endowment). Today, land grants have been replaced by annual $50,000 appropriations to each eligible college.

Before the name of East Lansing was ever considered, the mid/late-nineteenth century settlement that began to take shape around the intersection of what is today Michigan Avenue and Harrison Road was known as "Collegeville" (about 100 years later, at that same intersection, you can build your own burger at the Harrison Roadhouse, a tavern creating happiness since 1981).

Ray Stannard Baker was a journalist, a confidant of President Teddy Roosevelt, and Pulitzer Prize-winning biographer of President Woodrow Wilson. Ray Stannard Baker was also an area resident, born here in 1870, who wrote about early efforts to build the community: "We were very much in the country. It was a straggling, unorganized village, where we could know personally all our neighbors. At first there was no schoolhouse, no church… we all had to take hold and help: I did not know at the time how important this was. I was elected a school director, one of three, and we spent unnumbered hours planning and building the first schoolhouse in town. I learned much from this experience about how people work together in a democracy, all the more understandable because on so minute a scale."

Ray Stannard Baker's father-in-law was State Agricultural College (MSU) Professor William James Beal. In 1873, Professor Beal created an on campus outdoor laboratory for the study and appreciation of plants. The *W. J.*

Beal Botanical Gardens is the oldest continuously operated university botanical gardens in the United States, used and enjoyed today by students and by the general public alike. Besides its longevity, the W. J. Beal Botanical Gardens have been recognized as the outstanding campus-located botanical gardens in the country. Professor Beal's credits also include the first documented account of hybrid corn experimentation.

In 1898, University President Jonathan L. Snyder stated, "If we are compelled to have football, I like the kind that wins". The 119 to zero loss in 1902 to Fielding H. Yost and his UM point-a-minute team hurt, but it made it all the sweeter the 1913 MSU 12 to 7 victory in Ann Arbor, Michigan's only loss that year. The team came home to a jubilant celebration that included the burning of a barn on Grand River Avenue. Those who cannot remember the past are condemned to reheat it.

What do the Michigan cities of East Lansing and Omer have in common? Besides their location on the banks of fine paddling rivers (the Red Cedar and the Rifle, respectively), they have at one time had the distinction of being the state's smallest city: East Lansing when she achieved cityhood in 1907 (650 residents) and Omer today (295 residents).

The town's charter seeking cityhood went to the state legislature in 1907. The Michigan House approved the charter under the name of "College Park", while the Senate approved the charter under the name of "East Lansing". During the ensuing House-Senate debate, of course, East Lansing won out and, on May 8, 1907, the signature of Governor Fred Warner made cityhood official.

In East Lansing's charter was a section banning the sale or giving away of alcohol. This was the law until overturned by popular vote 61 years later, in 1968.

May of 1907 was a big month for the brand new city. On May 31, 1907, before a crowd of over 20,000, President Theodore Roosevelt gave the commencement speech at State Agricultural College. TR asked land grant colleges such as MSU to be at the forefront of extending to Michigan citizens the university's knowledge and resources to improve everyday living. The President's speech ignited the "Extension Service". In 1907, that meant teaching communities new farming or homemaking techniques. Today, MSU's Extension Service spreads its information base and assets throughout the state of Michigan, improving standards of living in all walks of life.

The East Lansing ambulance is laid up for repairs. All sick persons will kindly walk to the hospital until the driver, Dr. (Ward) Giltner, gives notice through this paper that the same is repaired. East Lansing Community Life, January 24, 1919.

Another reason why the women of East Lansing should vote: it took the United States tax experts one month to decide that a corset is not a luxury. East Lansing Community Life, May 23, 1919

Men's class at 12 Sunday. Professor Weaver begins a new series on the Bible. All men who can get permission from their wives are invited. East Lansing Community Life, September 30, 1920

A small band of gypsies have pitched their tents on the west side of River St., near Wm. Klever's house. We advise neighbors to keep their chicken coops locked. East Lansing Community Life, July 23, 1920

A prohibition-era story that was short, funny, and gave great insight into the times was this one told by East Lansing resident Robert Hicks. Robert was talking about his need for empty barrels to hold the cider that his orchard produced...

I got some of my barrels from the State Police. They confiscated illegal whiskey in barrels and would bring them in and dump the whiskey out in the Red Cedar River and leave the barrels along the river. Now, I needed barrels, and for fifty cents a barrel they'd sell them to me. I had an old gentleman helping me who had worked for the family for years and years. And sometimes he was quite talkative when he came back with a load of barrels. I asked him about it one day and he said, "You know, there's a pint or two left in the barrels". So he had a little supply all his own.

Depression-era union activity led to the 1937 "Battle of East Lansing". June sit-down strikes in Lansing auto plants led to the arrests of several area residents for "interfering in company operations". The union responded to the arrests by urging workers to declare a one day "labor holiday", demanding that all business be suspended for the day. The union activities were successful – until they tried to spread the shutdown to East Lansing. While going door to door in the business district with their demands that each store close for the day, the union men were soon followed by a crowd of jeering students. When one East Lansing shop refused to close and the union folks wouldn't accept that answer, the crowd of students threw the eight union men into the Red Cedar River while others overturned their cars. Back in Lansing, union leaders held a mass meeting on the steps of the capitol, letting their members know that "our boys are having a little trouble out at Michigan State College" and threatened to take over the campus. Several hundred factory workers marched to East Lansing where they were met by a crowd of students and townsfolk near the intersection of Michigan Avenue and Harrison Road. The "Battle of East Lansing" ensued with fists, clubs and two-by-fours. The outnumbered union men found themselves taking quite a pounding, with many more being tossed into the Red Cedar and the rest high-tailing it back to Lansing. The incident was well-covered in the national press, mostly in articles portraying the students and East Lansing residents as standing their ground against revolution.

The rich history of MSU has produced many firsts and other notable items including:

- Reaching into 83 Michigan counties through MSU Extension to provide practical, university-based knowledge.
- First in the nation for graduate programs in nuclear physics, industrial and organizational psychology, and rehabilitation counseling.
- First in the nation for graduate programs in elementary and secondary education.
- Leads the nation in study abroad participation among public universities.
- First USA major university with a dean of international programs.
- Ranks 4th among nation's largest universities in producing Peace Corps volunteers.
- One of the nation's top 5 campuses for sustainability, according to the National Wildlife Federation.
- Magic Johnson.
- Bell's Greek Pizza (grinders and pasta and pizza, oh my!)

THE TAVERN: DAGWOOD'S TAVERN & GRILL

When I sat down at Dagwood's and ordered my Pabst Blue Ribbon longneck, waitress Aly said, "Ooh that does sound good!" The wait staff here clearly knows quality.

The Red Cedar River seems to be giving the pub a hug, flowing south as it meanders below east-west Kalamazoo Road 1/4 mile to the bar's east, then turning west and wrapping itself south of the bar as it flows 1/4 mile away beneath the overpass of north-south US127. Pulling your canoe or kayak over on the Red Cedar shore and taking a 5-minute hike to Dagwood's would be a capital idea.

Although Dagwood's sits one block outside of the western edge of the East Lansing city limits, this is a classic campus pub. Great atmosphere, a funny & often feisty wait staff, and a menu with great old time tavern feeling that includes excellent burgers, chili, and navy bean & ham soup (the day I visited, for research purposes only, a letter arrived at Dagwood's asking for the navy bean & ham soup recipe).

As you enter Dagwood's, on your right is a phone booth without a phone ("they want way too much money to keep this working" says co-owner Mark). A partial history of the tavern has been scratched into the booth's wooden walls by customers down through the years. Next to the phone booth is a wonderful piece of artwork entitled "Pubs of Lansing" offering a subliminal outline of what would be a fine pub crawl.

Mark and Marji Cheadle have owned Dagwood's Tavern & Grill since 2000. Under their direction Dagwood's offers $1 PBRs each Monday from 7 'til close, so I have nothing bad to say about these two and their bar. In the interest of full disclosure, Mark paid for my burger 'n PBR, but I loved this place well before that magnanimous action

was taken.

Mark shares the bar's history with us…
Owner #1 of the bar named it "Trianon" after one of Marie Antoinette's palaces. He sold the tavern to owner #2, a gal who named the bar "Nims". Owner #3 bought the pub in 1947. He was a man named Durwood Root, better known to friends and patrons as "Dagwood". Dagwood was going to call the bar "The Garden", installing windows at booths (some still in place today) to create a bier garden look, but everyone kept referring to their favorite place by the owner's name, so "Dagwood's" it was and would remain. The rise in the back right corner was installed by Dagwood as a place where he could play his Hammond organ (just like Denny McLain, despite the fact that it's been said that there's never been any like Denny McLain) for customers. The back bar currently in place was built at and brought in from Bay City by Dagwood in 1947. In 1986, Dagwood sold his establishment to owner #4, Bob Lacea, and Bob sold it to the fifth and current owners, Mark and Marji, in 2000.

Dagwood's sells tshirts, sweatshirts and parkas with the name and address of the bar on the front. On the back, all share this wonderful quote by W.C. Fields, "I don't drink anymore, on the other hand I don't drink any less either".

Dagwood's is at 2803 E. Kalamazoo Street (1 block west of US127) in Lansing, phone (517) 374-0390

Sources: Jimmy Gretzinger, John Newman, Michigan State University, "At The Campus Gates" by Kestenbaum-Kuhn-Anderson-Green, Mark Cheadle

ROUGE & DETROIT RIVERS

Detroit MI

Trip: 5.1 miles/ 2 hours

Livery: Riverside Kayak Connection, 4016 Biddle Ave., Wyandotte MI 48192, phone number (734) 285-2925, www. riversidekayak.com. Owner – Tiffany Van DeHey.

Intermediate Ability

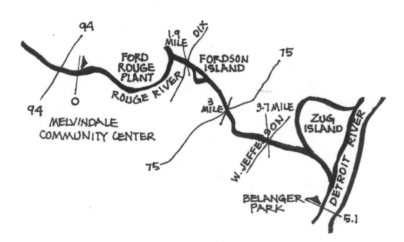

SOUNDTRACK: Rouge Plant Blues – Stix & Stones, Detroit '67 – Sam Roberts Band, Michigan & Trumbull – Ernie Harwell, Dancing in the Streets – Martha Reeves & the Vandellas, Motor City Baby – the Dirtbombs

RIVER QUOTE...
Maggie's take on the tall riverside mounds of salt, limestone and gravel, "It looks like we've arrived at the Detroit Rushmore".

MILES: zero mi from Detroit, 160 mi SE of Grand Rapids, 289 mi SE of Mackinaw City, 417 mi SE of Christmas, 374 mi E of Milwaukee.

THE BACKGROUND: ROUGE & DETROIT RIVERS

Paddling the Rouge River into the Detroit River is an amazing urban journey and a fascinating trip through history. Due to the depth of both rivers, and the rolling waters of the Detroit River, you should have at least intermediate paddling abilities before taking on this challenge. A surprise for many is the fact that wildlife thrives in this environment: blue herons, sandpipers, and hawks were among the birds spotted along the Rouge, and deer and fox were seen running across Fordson Island.

The Rouge River winds its way southeast for 126 miles, coming to an end as it merges with the 30-mile long and southwest flowing Detroit River. As the Rouge nears the Detroit River, it forms the southern border of the City of Detroit and the northern border of the town of River Rouge. Looking across the Detroit River you see Windsor, Canada. This is the only USA-Canada border site where, due to the unusual geography of the land, a Canadian city sits south of a United States city.

The trip outlined in this chapter is a two-hour paddle that takes you down the last 5 miles of the Rouge and less than one-half mile down the Detroit River. Before the trip

riverside communities to clean-up the river. Among many FOTR initiatives is their annual "Rouge Rescue", which has resulted in over 30,000 tons of trash and debris removed from the water. Restoring the Rouge is a work in progress, but due to the efforts of the Friends of the Rouge, recreational canoeing and kayaking has returned to this historic river. Their work is something that all Michigan residents can feel good about.

The health of a river can be gauged by the changes in the insect and fish population. In the Rouge, for the first time in decades, stone flies have hatched & salmon have spawned. For information on the Rouge, FOTR activities, and to see how you can help, go to www.therouge.org.

The Detroit River has a reputation as one of the best rivers in all of North America for the variety of fish found including walleye, small & largemouth bass, catfish, sturgeon, trout, pike, musky, crappies, freshwater drum, and suckers. *Steve's Bait Shop*, famous among Detroit River fishermen and the oldest bait shop in the city, is east of downtown at 6440 Jefferson Avenue at Meldrum, one street west of Belle Isle; phone (313) 259-1176.

The crack researchers paddling the Rouge & Detroit in September were the Friends of the Rouge, Tiffany Van DeHey & Riverside Kayak Connection, Maggie and Doc.

is 30 minutes old, you'll pass by the upstream edge of the Ford Motor Company's *Rouge Complex*. The first Model A Ford rolled off of this plant's assembly line in 1927. The first mass-produced vehicle ever made was built at Ford's Rouge Complex. It wasn't a car or a truck – it was the Fordson Tractor. In the 1920s, Ford Rouge was considered the most technically and architecturally advanced industrial complex in the world, and the largest sitting on 2,300 riverside acres: 1 mile long and a mile & one-half wide.

Working to restore the health of the Rouge is the remarkable environmental group, *Friends of the Rouge*. Since their 1986 inception, they've worked with industry and

THE RIVERS:
PADDLING THE ROUGE &
THE DETROIT

Launch on the Rouge River at the Melvindale boat launch behind the Community Event Center at 4300 S. Dearborn Drive near Allen Road. Take out on the Detroit River at Belanger Park in the town of River Rouge.

.2 mi/5 min in: float beneath the Greenfield Avenue Bridge.

.9 mi/20 min in: Schaefer Avenue Bridge & 1/20th of a mile later is the Railroad Bridge.

1.25 mi/26 min in: on left shore is a large red corrugated steel building - the upstream edge of the Ford Motor Company Rouge Complex.

1.6 mi/33 min in: on the left is the main body of the Ford Rouge complex.

1.7 mi/35 min in: to your left is the Rouge canal, also known as the "turning basin".

1.9 mi/41 min in: paddle beneath the Dix Avenue Drawbridge.

2 mi/44 min in: reach the upstream tip of Fordson Island. Going right at the island puts you on the path of the original Rouge River route. Going left at the island tip takes you down a man-made channel, one that is straight, deep and wide enough to accommodate ore carriers delivering raw materials to the Ford Motor Rouge complex.

Following the right fork around Fordson Island is the suggested route. It is fascinating viewing. Decades-old abandoned and partially-sunken boats dot the river here. The 8.4 acre island was created in 1917 or 1922 (depending on which respected source you use) when a request of the Ford Motor Co. was met to create a wider and deeper channel (i.e. the left river split at the 2 mile mark) than that offered by the Rouge River itself, and an island was born. Access to the island was possible by boat and a one-lane plank bridge (which still exists today) from Southwest Detroit. In the 1920s, lots were purchased on the newly-created island and riverfront homes were built. The last residents moved off of Fordson Island in 1989.

2.3 mi/52 min in: the river, on the right flow around Fordson Island, has narrowed to 10' across. Here very little clearance, 4' on our September trip, from river surface to bottom of the bridge exists to pass beneath the small plank bridge (our canoes and kayaks barely squeezed through). Check with Riverside Kayak Connection for the bridge clearance space on the day of your float. Once you've floated beneath this bridge, notice on your right a number of recreational boats docked, in various states of disrepair (in the 1950s, the Dearborn Yacht Club was located here).

2.35 mi/55 mi in: reach the downstream tip of Fordson Island.

2.55 mi/1 hr exactly: Just before the Fort Street Bridge, *Fresh Booze on the Rouge*, an old-time neighborhood tavern, is on your right (see "Taverns" section of this chapter). There is a dock at the river's edge which allows you to pull over for a little pub 'n grub.

2.6 mi/1 hr 1 min in: float beneath the Fort Street Bridge. A large salt storage pile is just downstream on your left. To your right lies the Marathon Ashland Petroleum Terminal &

Asphalt Plant.

3 mi/1 hr 10 min in: just past the railroad bridge, float below the I-75 Expressway Bridge.

3.3 mi/1 hr 17 min in: an impressively large railroad drawbridge is kept in an upright position on the left bank. You'll float by mounds of limestone, salt, and gravel.

3.55 mi/1 hr 23 min in: on the right is the U.S. Steel sign at the downstream end of the USS complex.

3.7 mi/1 hr 27 min in: pass below Jefferson Avenue Bascule Bridge (i.e. drawbridge).

4.2 mi/1 hr 36 min in: reach the upstream edge of Zug Island. The original Rouge channel flows left

around the island. Our suggested trip takes you to the right at the island's tip, floating the canal cut in 1888 (known as "the short cut canal") to establish a more direct route from the Rouge River to the Detroit River than the river's original path. This 1888 cut was enlarged in the 1920s at the request of Henry Ford to allow big ships easier passage to the Ford Rouge complex.

4.4 mi/1 hr 40 min in: float beneath the Zug Island Drawbridge.

4.8 mi/1 hr 50 min in: the Rouge empties into the Detroit River. Canada is straight ahead and the Ambassador Bridge is

in the distance on your left. As you turn right, merging from the Rouge to the Detroit River, you're rounding the northeast edge of the Detroit Edison Power Plant. On the western shore of the Detroit River are DTE-created Tern nesting platforms.

For the 3/10s of a mile that you'll be in the Detroit River, stay close to the right (western) shore & away from the large ships that traverse the river.

5.1 miles/ 2 hours – you're in! Arrive at Belanger Park in the town of River Rouge. Steer your boat between the large orange stanchions on your right and to the exit at the dock or ramp.

THE TOWN: DETROIT

Detroit Tiger local radio affiliate: WXYT 1270AM & 97.1FM

Yes, it is true that Detroit is known as the Motor City, Motown, the town that put the world on wheels.

No, it is not true that French explorer Cadillac, the European founder of Detroit, was named after the car. He did, however, have a larger and roomier canoe than everyone else, creating a higher standard.

The year 1701 Antoine de la Mothe Cadillac and his party, paddling canoes down the Detroit River, chose a riverside piece of land on the west side of the river as the site for his trading post. Cadillac established a settlement here and named it LaVille d'Etroit, "the City at the Straits". In 1752, the name was shortened to Detroit.

When the United States Government created the Michigan Territory in 1805, Detroit was named as the capital of the new territory. When Michigan was granted statehood in 1837, the once small settlement of LaVille d'Etroit was chosen as the new state's first capital.

Even before the advent of the automobile, Detroit was a manufacturing titan. In 1890, Detroit was the leading United States manufacturer of ships and rail cars. The city was also the largest producer of varnish and number 3 in the production of tobacco products. Then,

in 1896, Detroiter Charles Brady King built a car, the King Car. The first spin of the King Car was a drive on Jefferson and then Woodward. As wonderful as this new creation was, its cost was beyond that of the average person. And then came Ford.

In 1907, Henry Ford announced his plan to "create a motor car for the great multitude". His first step towards this goal was the 1908 introduction of the Model T: simple and sturdy, no fancy & expensive factory options offered, and available in any color as long as it was black. Yes, the Model T was less expensive than most any other car, but still priced beyond the means of the masses. Henry Ford

looked for a manufacturing method that would allow him to lower the cost to build and thus sell his Model T to everyman. Ford and his team, inspired by what they had seen of a grain mill's conveyor belt system, installed in 1913 the world's first – for large scale manufacturing - moving assembly line. The assembly line's interchangeable parts, continuous work flow, and division of labor meant lower production costs and a lower Model T price. The average citizen could now afford their own car. Henry Ford had realized his dream of putting the world on wheels and Detroit became universally known as (sing it CKLW) *"the Motor City"*.

Spurred by the success of its automotive industry, Detroit's population doubled between 1910 and 1920, reaching 1 million residents in 1920 (1.5 million including the suburbs) peaking at 1.9 million in 1950. Detroit & its suburbs formed the 4th largest metropolitan area in the USA in 1970 (4.8M population). From the twenties to the sixties, Detroit was frequently called the most cosmopolitan city in the Midwest, and "the Paris of America".

Assembly-line compensation provided workers with a very happy middle-class existence that often included a 2nd home getaway in the woods and on the lakes & rivers Up North.

Michigan & Trumbull, Michigan & Trumbull, there's never been a corner like Michigan & Trumbull from the 1999 song written by Ernie Harwell

In that same halcyon decade when the auto assembly line was created and Detroit's population doubled, there was also excitement at the corner of Michigan & Trumbull. In the winter of 1911-1912, the old wooden barn known as Bennett Park, where Ty Cobb & Sam Wahoo Crawford led the Detroit Tigers to American League pennants in 1907, 1908, and 1909, was torn down. In its place was built one of the first concrete and steel baseball parks in the country, Navin Field (eventually known as Briggs Stadium and then our beloved Tiger Stadium). The Tigers manager during those golden days (1907-1920) was Hughie "Ee-Yah!" Jennings. The popular Jennings managed the Tigers to victories in 1,131 games during his tenure, the team record until it was broken by (no, it wasn't Ralph Houk) one George Lee "Sparky" Anderson. Sparky managed the Tigers to 1,331 wins in his 17 (1979-1995) seasons. Perhaps even more popular than Jennings was in his day, Sparky frequently entertained us with his words of wisdom…

"Jose Conseco, he's built like a Greek goddess", "Every 24 hours the world turns over on someone who was sitting on top of it", "I only had a high school education & believe me, I had to cheat to get that", "The problem with John Wockenfuss getting on base is that it takes 3 doubles to score him", "Me carrying a briefcase is like a hot dog wearing earrings", "The great thing about baseball is when you're done, you'll only tell your grandchildren the good things. If they ask me about 1989, I'll tell 'em I had amnesia".

Since the sixties, Detroit has experienced severe erosion in manufacturing jobs, specifically those in auto and auto-related industries, in population (falling below 1M) and in its tax base. Once the national leader in worker per capita income and home ownership, the city is today among the USA's leaders in unemployment and home foreclosures. As the fortunes of Motown seem bleakest, resurgence begins.

That resurgence is driven in part by Detroit's Big 3 of Ford, GM & Chrysler. Their sales and profit rebound is a result of new 2nd to none quality products and vehicle designs that brings consumers into the showroom, gets 'em to open their wallets, and ultimately creates new jobs in the city. Detroit's renaissance is more than an automotive one, though.

Hope, creativity, and cool on another level are contributing to the city's comeback, led by young adults re-populating the city. An entrepreneurial spirit is at work, the ideas of small independents not choked out by the presence of national (non-automotive) corporations. In an economy standing on the lower rungs, these new Moms 'n Pops can and are quickly making a difference…

- *TechOne* is an incubator for high tech innovations and solutions
- *Russell Industrial Center* is the Midwest's largest harbor for small businesses and artists; its 150 commercial tenants include architects, graphic designers, clothing designers, filmmakers, craftsmen and sculptors
- *NextEnergy* drives alternative energy growth through research, testing and consulting.
- *Omni Corp* supports experimentation and collaboration in technology, electronics and art; they provide an extension service to the community through learning and workshop sessions.

Seems like a good time to recall one other Sparky quote: "People who live in the past generally are afraid to compete in the present. I've got my faults, but living in the past is not one of them. There's no future in it".

Area camping: the Wayne County Fairgrounds, 23 miles from the Belanger Park take-out, are the nearest campgrounds. The address is 10871 Quirk Road in Belleville 48111; phone (734) 697-7002. See www.waynecountyfairgrounds.net.

THE TAVERN: FRESH BOOZE ON THE ROUGE

It's always a treat when you can access an old time tavern by paddling right up to it, and "Fresh Booze on the Rouge" (aka the Bridge Café) is one of those taverns. 2 and one-half miles into the float, one hour of steady paddling, you'll see Fresh Booze sitting on the right bank just before the Fort Street Bridge. Pull your boat over, tie up at the dock, and the bar is just a few feet away. For those driving, the tavern is at the intersection of Fort St. & Oakwood, just south of the Rouge River (a few blocks south of Miller).

Fresh Booze on the Rouge opened in 1936, a great time to be a Michigan sports fan...

- opening just a few months after the Detroit Tigers celebrated their first World Series win in October of 1935, Goose Goslin knocks in Mickey Cochrane, bottom of the 9th in game 6, to defeat the Chicago Cubs,
- and the bar opened even fewer months after the Detroit Lions won their first NFL Championship in the Fall of '35,
- and just a few weeks after the Detroit Red Wings took their first Stanley Cup, defeating the Toronto Maple Leafs in the Spring of '36,
- and it was Detroit's own Brown Bomber, Joe Louis, who in 1935 at Yankee Stadium defeated in the boxing ring Max Baer – the same Max Baer who's son, Max Baer Junior, went on to play Jethro Bodine in the *Beverly Hillbillies* (isn't it funny how the circle of life always comes back to the *Beverly Hillbillies?*).

Owner Chris is a friendly sort, having taken over the bar in 1999 from his Dad, who bought it in 1980. Chris tells us that Fresh Booze first went under the name of Brown's Bar when its doors opened in 1936. Before the tavern was erected, this was the location of a fire pumping station, bringing in water from the Rouge to fight neighborhood fires.

This is a classic neighborhood tavern. Indentations in each seat, varying in size and shape based on the derriere of each regular, lets you know who that seat belongs to. Stop in to stretch your river legs, quench your thirst, grab a bite, shoot some pool, throw darts, play a tune on the juke box, or just soak in a little old-time Dee-troit neighborhood history.

Fresh Booze On The Rouge is at 130 S. Fort Street in Detroit, phone (313) 406-5325.

THE TAVERN "BONUS": TOM'S TAVERN

Long-time Tom's patron Matthew Rose shares these memories of his old Detroit neighborhood tavern...

"The less that you bothered owner Tom in ordering beer or food, the less your bill. He encouraged you to get your own beer from the cooler and drop your plates in the sink. The last patron to leave at night had to drive Tom home (I did it twice – he lived over on Outer Drive). The floors were so slanted and uneven, the bar stools were cut at different heights to make things look more uniform. I heard that the old man, Tom, died a number of years ago. He was a piece of work".

Tom's is located at 10093 W. 7 Mile Road at Wyoming, Detroit, ph (313) 862-9768

Sources: Sally Petrella, Tiffany Van DeHey, Dearbornarealiving.com, Chris Weaks, www.historydetroit. com, www.pbs.org, Detroit Free Press, Southeast Michigan StartUp, Detroit Lives, Baseball Almanac, Matthew Rose

ST. JOSEPH RIVER
Hillsdale MI
Trip 3.8 miles/ 1 hour
& 40 minutes

Canoes & Kayaks supplied by: G.R.E.A.T. Grand River
Environmental Action Team, P.O. Box 223, Jackson MI 49204,
(517) 416-4234, www.great-mi.org.

Intermediate Ability

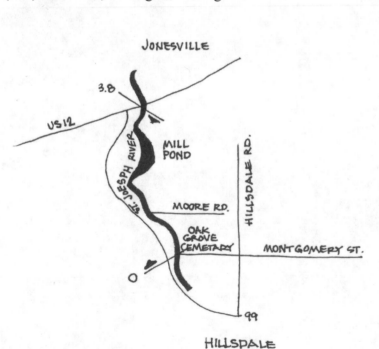

SOUNDTRACK: Toes (Life is Good Today, a PBR on the way) – Zach Brown Band, Time Has Come Today – Chambers Brothers, Pitkin County Turnaround – Steve Martin, Cry Me a River – Dinah Washington, Caisson Song (over hill, over dale) – the U.S. Army

RIVER QUOTE...
Kathy Kulchinski: "Every minute on the water is *fun!*"

MILES: 94 mi SW of Detroit, 126 mi SE of Grand Rapids, 289 mi S of Mackinaw City, 417 mi SE of Christmas, 282 mi SE of Milwaukee WI (birthplace of PBR)

THE BACKGROUND: ST. JOSEPH RIVER

The St. Joseph River is Michigan's 3rd longest river at 210 miles long. Its headwaters are just SE of Hillsdale, flowing down from Baw Beese Lake. From there, the river follows a jagged line mostly west and then a bit south as it drops briefly into Indiana near Elkhart before turning NW until it empties out into Lake Michigan at the town of St. Joseph, MI. Along its 210 miles the river falls 600'.

Working to keep the river and its watershed clean are *The Friends of the St. Joe River*. Formed in 1994, the group coordinates efforts in communities both along the river and within the St. Joseph watershed to maintain the health of the river and the lakes and streams within the watershed. See www.fotsjr.org.

The trip outlined here has its beginnings in Hillsdale, near the St. Joseph's headwaters, where the river is a narrow 10' wide. Hearing that any section of this river could be that narrow would come as a surprise to most folks who only know the St. Joe through their I94 drives in SW Michigan, where they cross over a river 100' wide. Experiencing the dramatic size difference at a river's headwaters versus further downstream, especially a river that is overwhelmingly identified as so big & wide, is part of the fun of paddling a river at its small stream origins.

This river trip flows north from Hillsdale until reaching the take out at the US12 Bridge in Jonesville. Please note that this voyage was taken just two days after a 3" rain, with the result of a significantly higher water level and faster current flow than normal.

The stretch of the St. Joseph River in this chapter receives a degree of difficulty rating of *intermediate* due to (1) deadwood obstructions along the river's narrow headwaters, (2) the deep mud at Mill Pond, and (3) the portage required at the dam.

The fishing in the St. Joe includes steelhead, smallmouth bass, walleye, salmon and brown trout.

Crack researchers on the St. Joseph River in May were members of two paddling and environmental groups: G.R.E.A.T. (Jim Seitz, Kenny Price, Kathy Kulchinski, Pegg Clevenger and Ben Whiting) and the Great Lakes Paddlers (Tom and Sharon Brandau), plus Rod & Jackie Mona Smith, Karen & Jeff Cripe, Maggie and Doc.

THE RIVER: PADDLING THE ST. JOSEPH

Launch in Hillsdale at the Montgomery Road Bridge, an old wooden bridge just west of the Oak Ridge Cemetery. To get to the launch site, take M99 to just north of Hillsdale, then E on Fayette Road, N on West Road, and W on Montgomery Road to the river.

Immediately upon launching you have to keep on your toes as the river winds quickly past deadwood that blocks half of the water's 10' width. One kayak in our large flotilla flips within 30' of launching, immediately creating a bottleneck.

.5 mi/12 min: from the right a creek merges. You float

beneath a canopy of trees from launch until the 1 mile mark.

1 mi/23 min: river widens to 25'. The tree cover is gone & you paddle below open skies.
The water has deepened from 2' to 4'.

1.2 mi/26 min: very marshy flatland surrounds you. Cattails abound and the nearest trees lie 100 yards beyond the riverbanks.

1.3 mi/29 min: river widens to 60'. Two silos (from "Silos Fun Park") are visible far to your left (west) at M99.

1.6 mi/35 min: river tightens to 25' wide and trees return to the river banks. A beaver swims in front of our canoe to the right shore.

1.7 mi/38 min: paddle beneath the Moore Road Bridge. Beyond the bridge, the river's speed enjoys a 5 minute surge (2.3 to 4 mph). The surge ends as the river widens to 50'.

2.1 mi/45 min: on right shore is the first house seen on this stretch of the river. Lily pads are suddenly everywhere. You are now floating into Mill Pond.

2.4 mi/50 min: on the right shore is the 2nd home seen today. Bass are thrashing around among the lily pads. Maggie speculated that they were spawning 'cause she smelled fish. Mill Pond has widened to 200' across.

River Warning!...

2.7 mi/55 min: immediately after the lily pads, stay right of midstream! To the left and below the river's surface is mud that is like quicksand. During a river race just days before our float, a kayak came to a stop on the mud. When the kayaker stepped out of his boat to push it through, he sank in mud to his armpits. ***Stay in your boat!***

2.9 mi/57 min: a homeowner's single hole golf course is beyond the right shore.

3 mi/1 hour: arrive at the dam. The river narrows as it flows left. There is a portage at the hill just past the bay on the right. Be careful of the small culvert sitting at the far right of the bay: there is a surprisingly strong current pulling you towards the culvert, and one of our flotilla kayaks got sucked through (the kayaker was rescued).

3.3 mi/1 hr 8 min: downstream from the dam, you're deep into a beautiful bayou country with many Maple trees dotting the landscape. You meander through sweet flowing S-curves. The water is well over paddle length deep and 30' wide.

3.5 mi/1 hr 12 min: a home is just beyond the left bank.

3.8 mi/1 hr 20 min: you're in! Take out on the left shore, just before the US 12 Bridge in Jonesville. There's a nice, gradual slope here that makes it easy to take your canoe or kayak out. Looking over the front tip of your beached boat is a McDonald's. How many paddlers have used their bathroom over the years? Something about the golden arches…

Across the river, on the right shore, is a nice picnic area for post-paddling relaxation.

THE TOWN: HILLSDALE

Detroit Tiger local radio affiliate: WCSR 1340AM

Over hill, over dale, on the canoe & kayak trails is a slight modification of the official song of the United States Army, but an appropriate modification for the town of Hillsdale and the county (also called Hillsdale) in which it resides:

- The "Hillsdale" name derives from its terrain of both *hills* and *dales* (valleys).
- Hillsdale County's hills (peaking at 1,250' above sea level) provide the high ground from which flow the headwaters for five major rivers (fine canoe & kayak

trails): the St. Joseph, the Kalamazoo, the Grand, the Raisin, and a 2nd St. Joseph River, this one flowing south to a merger with Ohio's Maumee River.

The town of Hillsdale, 18 miles north of the Michigan-Ohio border, is centrally located within Hillsdale County and is its county seat. A fun fact to regale your friends with over a Pabst is that Hillsdale County is the only Michigan county that borders two states, Ohio and Indiana. The county has a monument located at the most extreme southern point in Michigan, where the boundaries of Michigan, Indiana and Ohio meet.

Baw Beese Lake is the name of the lake from which the waters of the St. Joseph River begin. The lake's name resulted from the admiration that residents of Hillsdale had for Chief Baw Beese, the leader of the area's tribe of Potawatomi Indians. As the earliest white settlers entered Hillsdale in the 1820s and 30s, Baw Beese and his band assisted them through difficult times and seasons by providing food and medical care. A family atmosphere was said to exist among the Native Americans and the settlers, extremely rare at the time. This happy situation lasted until 1840 when a local pioneer purchased land & wrote a letter to President Harrison. The letter requested federal government help, under the 1830 *Indian Removal Act*, in ejecting the Chief and his people from land that the pioneer purchased. Although against the wishes of the overwhelming majority of the local community, federal troops arrived to remove the tribe from the county. With a heavy heart, the townsfolk came out of their homes, even taking their kids out of school, to say goodbye to Chief Baw Beese & his folk as they were forced, under escort of federal troops, to a reservation near Topeka, Kansas. There's no happy ending here.

The North Country National Scenic Trail (NCNST), a 4,600 mile footpath linking North Dakota to New York, passes through Hillsdale County. Walking the trail is a wonderful way to see the area's natural beauty. The footpath enters the county through Ohio before moving northwest through the Lost Nations State Game Area and then through the towns of Hillsdale and Jonesville. The Hillsdale County Chapter of the NCNST is responsible for developing and maintaining that portion of the trail that lies within the county. In another tribute to the memory of a deserving individual, the Hillsdale County Chapter is known by the name of the Chief Baw Beese Chapter.

Hillsdale College, founded in 1844, is a central part of the town's life. Although the college is small in size with an enrollment of 1,300 students, it is known nationally for its refusal of taxpayer subsidies to cover any of its costs, and for its publication of the magazine *Imprimis* (1.9M monthly readers), a reflection of conservative thinking.

Michigan's poet laureate, Will Carleton, was a graduate at Hillsdale College. As a college student in the 1860s, Will was a frequent visitor to a house & farm maintained as a home for the aged and the infirm whose families would no longer care for them, the Hillsdale County Poor House. In 1872, Will wrote about the sad plight of this home's residents in his poem, *"Over the Hill to the Poor House"*. Almost immediately upon its publication, the poem and its author became a national sensation. Across the country, attention was focused on, and action taken to, improve

the lot of aging folks in need. A movie on the subject, also called "Over the Hill to the Poor House", was one of the most popular movies of its times. The spotlight on the subject begun by Will Carleton's poem may have been the catalyst eventually resulting in the United States adopting Social Security (think about that again: the poem of a Hillsdale College graduate might have lead to Social Security). Almost from the moment that "Over the Hill to the Poor House" was published, Will Carleton became one of the most popular writers and lecturers in our country, a position that Will maintained until he passed away in 1912. The Hillsdale house that inspired Will's poem is today called the *Will Carleton Poor House.* It is listed on the National and State Register of Historic Sites, and is open to the public as a museum maintained by the Hillsdale County Historical Society.

Area camping: 3 Hillsdale area options (1) Gateway Park Campground on South Sand Lake www.gatewayparkcampground.com; 517-437-7005), (2) Sugarbush Campground on 2571 S. Sand Lake Rd www.sugarbushcampground.com; 517-398-4919), and (3) 6 Lakes Campground located on Boot Lake www.6lakescampground.com; 517-439-5660.

THE TAVERN #1: THE HUNT CLUB

The highbrow name, along with the bar's appearance from outside, belies the old time pub comfort found inside the tavern walls. The Hunt Club serves its customers out of a structure built in 1871 and it honors that history. A large portion of the building's original brick wall is still visible inside the bar. The 1871 tin ceiling, in all its gorgeous detail, still remains in place. The interior lighting puts you at ease, providing its patrons with a comfortable "yes I'll have another" darkness even on a sunny afternoon (making it easy to forget time and responsibilities in the outside world).

The Hunt Club is known for excellent Rueben sandwiches and burgers. Tavern Manager Marsha said that customers tell her these are the best burgers in town. I can personally attest to their goodness: my burger was delicious and adding condiments would have been a waste – they were *that* tasty. The burger came with a side of really, really good homemade crunchy chips. Rounding out the menu is a long list of sandwiches, steaks, fish, burritos, appetizers, soups and salads.

Not all is nirvana at The Hunt Club: Pabst, the 1893 winner of the Blue Ribbon at the Chicago World's Fair, is not available (maybe if I lived in Hillsdale that would change). However, bottles of Stroh's are on hand (an excellent plan B) and 14 oz. Labatt's are $1.50 all day, every day.

Upstairs is its own bar, open for special events like charity poker, a Thursday through Sunday Hunt Club happening. A disc jockey occasionally entertains on the main floor.

The Hunt Club has been the elegant building's tenant since 1989, the same year that the back bar was installed. The interior refurbishing of the bar was handled by the previous occupant, Sherlock's Tavern. For years before 1986, this was home to the Hub Cigar Bar, which Marsha says was not a cigar bar, per se, and was a place where everyone helped themselves to drinks (an honor system in place) except the fairer sex: women were not welcomed at the Hub Cigar Bar. Within 3 years of this policy change, the Berlin Wall came tumbling down. *Ich bin ein Hillsdaler.*

The Hunt Club is at 24 N. Howell, across the street from the County Courthouse in downtown Hillsdale, phone (517) 437-7356

THE TAVERN #2: SAUCY DOG'S BARBEQUE

Located in downtown Jonesville, one-half block east of where the St. Joe flows beneath the US12 Bridge (i.e. the end of the suggested trip), is the Saucy Dog's Barbeque bar.

Great Barbeque is what they do! The Saucy menu features pulled pork, smoked chicken, beef brisket, and the St. Louis rib sampler (7 finger-lickin' Saucy Dog's ribs tossed in sweet barbeque sauce), which can be topped off by a Carmel Apple Sundae (mm-mm).

As it is with the Hunt Club, you should be aware that Saucy's lies within Hillsdale County, where hard liquor is not served on Sundays. Pabst is not served at Saucy's any day of the week, but fortunately *that* situation could be changed without a revision to the law.

There is a noticeable lack of video games, darts, pool tables, etc. You come to Saucy's and it's just you, your friends, great food, and conversing about your day on the river (which can all be enjoyed on the back deck, if you choose).

Dog-lovers make their statements at Saucy's beneath the polyurethane covered bar top with wisdom like… "The more I know about men, the more I love my dog" & "Anyone who says he works like a dog doesn't own one". Mixed drinks have names that include 4-Legged Friend, Pink Poodle, Lap Dog, My Sweet Husky, The Boxer, and Isaboo's Muddy Paw (with Frangelico, Bailey's, Kahlau, & coffee topped with whipped cream).

The Saucy Dog's Barbeque is at 212 E. Chicago Road (US12), just east of the river, in Jonesville, ph (517) 849-2272.

Sources: GREAT, Great Lakes Paddlers, Friends of St. Joe River, Hillsdalehistory.com, Hunt Club Manager Marsha, Mitchell Research Center's Betty Beaubien & Janis Reister, Hillsdalecounty.info, Hillsdale County Chamber of Commerce

SHIAWASSEE RIVER
Holly MI
Trip 6.6 miles/ 3 hours

Intermediate Ability

Livery: Fairbanks Canoes & Kayaks, Linden MI 48451, (810) 287-9618. Owners Doug and Kristy Fairbanks.

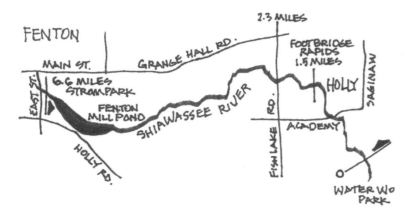

SOUNDTRACK: Good Time – Alan Jackson, Who's To Say – Blanche, Chirpy ChirpyCheep Cheep – Mac & Katie Wissoon, Seven Nation Army – the White Stripes, The Shiawassee's Song – Mary Carruthers, Go Get 'Em Tigers! – the State of Michigan

RIVER QUOTE...
Doc: "Darn, I missed that photo op", Colonel Braun: "There's always a second chance", Karen Braun: "Unless there isn't"

MILES: 54 mi NW of Detroit, 126 mi East of Grand Rapids, 238 mi SE of Mackinaw City, 366 mi SE of Christmas, 375 mi East of Milwaukee

THE BACKGROUND: SHIAWASSEE RIVER

The Shiawassee River flows for 110 miles north/northwest through the southeast Lower Peninsula. Near the end of its journey, it merges with the Flint River, the Cass River, and the Titabawassee River in the Shiawassee National Wildlife Refuge, known locally as Shiawassee Flats. The merger of these four rivers forms the Saginaw River, which then flows north into Saginaw Bay.

The Shiawassee meanders through the towns of Holly, Fenton, Linden, Argentine, Owosso and Chesaning on its way to Shiawassee Flats. Recreational use of the river has increased greatly since the 2000s. Due in large part to the efforts of the paddling and environmental groups *Headwaters Trails Inc* and their sister volunteers at the *Keepers of the Shiawassee*, the first 40 miles of the lower Shiawassee, from Holly to Argentine, is open to kayakers and canoers. Their river activities include chain sawing obstructions, trash pick-up, and anchoring logs to the river banks for the benefit of fish habitat. One long term goal of *Headwaters* and *Keepers* is to open the river to paddlers along its entire length, from Holly to the Shiawassee Flats.

These two groups schedule paddling events, river clean-ups, installation of stream side signage, and establish canoe & kayak launch sites. Their efforts have brought Up North river experiences to within 60 to 90 minutes of Detroit and her suburbs. For further information on both groups and on the Shiawassee River, check out their websites: www: headwaterstrailsinc.org and www.keepersof the shiawassee. com.

The Shiawassee River trip outlined in this chapter launches in Holly near the river's headwaters and ends almost 7 miles (a 3 hour paddle) downstream in Fenton. The Holly put-in is at WaterWorks Park at 602 Broad Street. The Fenton take-out is at Strom Park at 299 South East Street. The source of the Shiawassee is Mill Pond which narrows at its west end before widening into Stiffs Mill Pond. It is from the west end of Stiffs Mill Pond that the Shiawassee River begins its journey near WaterWorks Park.

The 3 hour trip has frequent deadwood paddling challenges, a gorgeous and cooling canopy overhead from trees leaning in from both banks, culverts (tunnels) to paddle through, a few rapids runs in the early going, and many sightings of swans, geese, ducks, and beavers.

Fishermen encountered on the river caught pike, largemouth bass, bluegill, and crappies.

Crack researchers paddling the Shiawassee River in early June were Greg & Pam Palinsky, Teresa Salem, the Braun Family 5 of the Colonel, Julie, Eric (aka "Milford Slims"), Karen and Big Joe, Andy Kocembo, Paula Brown, Maggie and Doc.

THE RIVER: PADDLING THE SHIAWASSEE

Launching at the WaterWorks access in Holly, the river is 2'

deep, as it will remain most of the day, and 15' wide with a marsh on the left and tall trees to your right.

.2 mi/5 min: float through the dual culverts at *LeGrande Road*. You're paddling past many Holly homes along the right shore.

.6 mi/17 min: an impressive oak tree is along the right bank with a home behind it; just beyond as the river bends left, railroad tracks sit atop the right bank bluff.

.8 mi/22 min: the forest on the left has a haunting dark beauty to it; ahead you'll paddle below a small pedestrian bridge.

.9 mi/24 min: the river speeds up nicely as you float through a fun little culvert, requiring single file paddling to get through it.

1 mi/25 min: pass a "1 mile" marker on the left shore. We saw one each mile except at the 4 and 6 mile marks. A sign alerts you to the "fast current/low culverts ahead".

Around the very next bend is a triple culvert beneath a railroad bed. The sign one bend upstream was accurate: there is only a 2' clearance from the top of our canoes and kayaks to the bottom of the culvert roof.

Warning: in times of high water levels (springtime, after heavy rains) getting through these culverts could be dangerous.

1.2 mi/31 min: as the river turns right, a dead creek merges left.

1.3 mi/32 min: a right bank sign recaps the turning point of the 1972 Clean Water Act in improving the health of the Shiawassee River and all of the efforts since then, noting that the "bad old days are gone". For this sign and those at the WaterWorks put-in, the Strom Park take-out, the mile markers, etc., we can thank the folks at Headwaters Trails Inc.

1.4 mi/35 min: a midstream island creates left/right passing corridors only 5' wide, surroundings similar to that of the Fox River spreads in the U.P.

1.5 mi/41 min: the "portage" sign on the left bank directs you to a 40' long shoreline path OR you can paddle through the very fun rapids, tumbling over the rocks and beneath the footbridge.

1.7 mi/47 min: "2 mile" marker is on the left. The tree canopy formed above is amazing.

2 mi/53 min: at a right river bend, a big creek merges from the

left.

2.2 mi/1 hr: a sign announces a *crane nesting site.*

2.3 mi/1 hr: a single culvert takes you below *Fish Lake Road*; there is a small access at the Fish Lake Road Bridge.

2.8 mi/1 hr 19 min: pass the "3 mile" marker on your left. The canopy of leaning trees has been replaced by lowland grass along both shores; turkey vultures circle above.

3.1 mi/1 hr 28 min: pass beneath a railroad trestle enveloped on all sides by cat tails and water lilies.

3.6 mi/1 hr 44 min: after 30 minutes of treeless, grassy banks, you're again paddling through the dark beauty of a riverside forest.

3.7 mi/1 hr 47 min: the river widens into a large bay 200' wide and 100' long; here there is a little sandy beach on the right, a nice place to pull the boats over and take a break. Stay to the left as you paddle into the bay. Once out of the bay, the river narrows to 40', much wider than it was at the upstream side of the bay. On the shoreline, barren trees and water lilies predominate.

4.1 mi/2 hrs: the river suddenly narrows to 10'; bushes reach out to you from each river bank. There are large trees behind the bushes. It is exquisite here floating below nature's canopy.

4.4 mi/2 hrs 9 min: paddle below the power lines.

4.7 mi/2 hrs 15 min: at the tip of a short oxbow lies a sandy beach, a fine break spot as the river bends to the right. You soon encounter a series of small islands. Geese, ducks and swans are all around and very active.

5 mi/2 hrs 23 min: "5 mile" marker is on the right bank. You are no longer beneath the canopy of trees. Pass below the power lines and see a home on the right.

5.4 mi/2 hrs 30 min: on your right, the field of water lilies seems to stretch forever.

5.7 mi/2 hrs 40 min: enter the very wide waters of the Fenton Mill Pond and paddle to the right. Keep in mind that within the pond there is no current at your back, so you'll be in for 20 minutes of good exercise until the take-out. Once in the pond, the deeper water on your left is easier to paddle. In the pond we saw, gathered together swimming in one 10' area, 3 adult geese with 25 baby gray geese.

<u>Do NOT</u> go through the quadruple culverts at East Street. Paddle towards the take-out point to the left of the East Street culverts.

6.6 miles/3 hours: you're in! The Strom Park access is on the left.

THE TOWN: HOLLY

Detroit Tigers local radio affiliate: WTRX 1330AM

Holly is located within an hour drive of many Detroit suburbs. It's a small town with friendly folks, a quaint downtown, and some fascinating history.

Battle Alley is Holly's 1800s historic district and its street and shops have a distinctly turn-of-the-last-century feel about them. The street name was changed from Martha Street to Battle Alley after a wild 1880 brawl between a riled up group of local gents and some workers from a traveling circus that left most of the brawl's participants severely beaten and/or jailed.

Within Battle Alley is the famous Holly Hotel. An early-1900s incident at the Holly Hotel solidified the *Battle Alley* name. On August 28, 1908, the Kansas saloon smasher herself, Miss Carry Nation, and her pro-temperance friends paid a visit to the Holly Hotel. Carry entered the Holly Hotel's very large bar and began smashing whiskey bottles with her trademark hatchet, while her friends clubbed bar patrons over the head with their umbrellas. The net result of Carry Nation's rampage was to bring long-lasting notoriety to the Holly Hotel bar and a night in jail for Carry. Over 100 years later, the Holly Hotel continues to annually celebrate that long-ago visit of Carry Nation with a re-enactment of her visit and, naturally, specially-reduced prices on alcoholic beverages.

The history of the Holly Hotel includes a devastating 1978 fire, a fire so bad that the town's last architectural link to the 1800s was considered for demolition. Instead, the needed funding was raised and reconstruction took place with painstaking detail to the original 1891 drawings. Every piece of the hotel which survived the 1978 fire was incorporated into the project. One of the many fascinating details of this effort was the fact that the reconstructed back bar was built using materials saved from the very first Cunningham Drug Store in Detroit (built in 1889). Two years after the 1978 fire, the rebuilt Holly Hotel was as fabulous as ever, and on February 8, 1980, the Holly Hotel was entered into the USA's National Register of Historic Places.

"The largest piano factory on earth", as it was known to the proud residents of Holly, was opened 1913 in Holly by Grinnell's Piano. Grinnell's had a reputation for top-of-the-line quality and in the 1950s their location in little Holly became the world's largest piano factory and distribution center. Many Holly-built pianos were shipped over the years to their warehouse near Tiger Stadium at 2003 Brooklyn Street. Today, that Detroit warehouse has been transformed into living space known as the "Grinnell Lofts".

Holly has a couple of noteworthy connections to our fighting men and women…

• Born and raised in Holly was Karl Richter, an officer in the United States Air Force and a fighter pilot during the Vietnam War. At the age of 23, Karl had the distinction of being the youngest pilot in that conflict to shoot down a MiG (a Russian-built fighter jet) in air-to-air combat. His skill and heroic actions, on that day and many others, earned him a Silver Star, Air Force Cross, Distinguished Flying Cross, and Bronze Star. Karl Richter died in action in 1967. In 1992, a statue of Karl was unveiled at Maxwell Air Force Base in Montgomery, Alabama.

• In 2005, the Department of Veteran Affairs established the Great Lakes National Cemetery in Holly Township. The cemetery is north of town and borders Fagan Lake. This is one of only 130 in the national cemetery system, reserved primarily for veterans and members of the armed forces, and reserves and National Guard members. Our dear paddling brother Wayne Thomas Vollmers, R.I.P. 11.16.08, United States Army, Vietnam veteran, is buried here. 4Day Wayne-O!

KaBOOM! is a national non-profit dedicated to building and renovating playgrounds in the USA. They have designated Holly as a "Playful City USA," one of the country's 150 best communities for providing its kids with access to playground space. Get the kids away from their tech trance and out doors doing what they do best – play.

Countless studies over the years show that play time equates to healthier, happier, smarter and more social kids. KaBOOM! tells us that Holly has what kids need.

Area camping: the Flint/Holly KOA Campground (also known as the Holly Fun! Park) is just NE of Holly, off I-75 exit 101. The address is 7072 E. Grange Road in Holly 48442; phone (248) 634-0803.

THE TAVERN: BLACKTHORN PUB

Holly has what adults need, too: a fine Irish tavern called Blackthorn Pub.

The structure housing Blackthorn's was built in 1865. What better way to commemorate the end of Irish brothers killing one another on different sides of the North-South divide, aka the Civil War, than to construct a place where differences can be settled, or at least ruminated upon, over a pint.

This place is a 30' wide by 80' long Irish shoebox full of fun! The joint was jumping on our visit, absolutely packed with folks having a blast. There is live entertainment on the weekends, but it's clear that Blackthorn's patrons don't need to wait for the weekend to have a good time.

Partners Rory Kelly and Ben Leahy opened the Blackthorn Pub in early-2011. Among the long line of bars and restaurants previously residing in this building, the last tenant prior to Blackthorn was known as Yosemite's.

Owners Rory and Ben give you plenty of whet your whistle options. You can choose from over 30 different kinds of Irish and Scottish whiskey. Blackthorn's also stocks 112 different beers in bottles and 20 on tap. The beers offered on tap are regularly rotated and always feature at least one "throwback" brand, along them Pabst and Schlitz (now we're talking!).

Blackthorn chefs are constantly working up new recipes, with dishes often created over drinks and video games, taste testing the various fares as they go to come up with new and delicious offerings that'll send everyone home fat, sassy and smiling.

Faith and begorrah, we <u>will</u> be back!

Blackthorn Pub is located at 105 S. Saginaw (a short walk from Battle Alley) in Holly MI 48442. Phone (248) 369-8714.

Sources: Headwaters Trails Inc., US Fish & Wildlife Service, www.hollyholel.com, Michigan Historic Site marker, www.air-forcemagazine.com, Rory Kelly

MICHIGAN CANOE & KAYAK LIVERIES

Listed alphabetically by river, first Upper Peninsula then Lower Peninsula

AUTRAIN RIVER

AuTrain River Canoe and Kayak Rental 906-892-8367
N7163 Forest Lake Rd, AuTrain, MI 49806
http://autrainrivercanoes.com

Northwoods Resort 906-892-8114
N7070 Forest Lake Rd, AuTrain, MI 49806
http://www.northwoodsresort.net/

BRULE RIVER

Michi-Aho Resort 906-875-3514
2181 M-69, Crystal Falls, MI 49920
http://www.michiahoresort.com/

Northwoods Wilderness Outfitters 906-774-9009, 1-800-530-8859
N-4088 Pine Mountain Road, Iron Mountain, MI 49801
http://www.northwoodsoutfitters.com/

CARP RIVER

U.P. Wide Adventure Guide 906-430-0547
W6508 Epoufette BayRoad, Naubinway, MI 49762
http://www.upwideadventureguide.com/

ESCANABA RIVER

Soaring Eagle Outfitters 906-346-9142, 877-346-9142
93 N. Pine Street, Gwinn, MI 49841
www.soaringeagleoutfitters.us

Uncle Ducky Outfitters 906-228-5447, 877-228-5447
434 E. Prospect, Marquette, MI 49855
http://www.uncleduckyoutfitters.com/

FORD RIVER

Mr. Rental 906-789-7776, 877-906-7776
627 Stephenson Ave., Escanaba, MI 49829

FOX RIVER

Big Cedar Campground & Canoe Livery 906-586-6684
7936 State Hwy. M-77, Germfask, MI 49836
http://www.bigcedarcampground.com/

Northland Outfitters 906-586-9801, 800-808-3FUN
8174 Hwy M-77, Germfask, MI 49836
http://www.northoutfitters.com/

LAKE SUPERIOR/PICTURED ROCKS

Northern Waters Adventures 906-387-2323
712 West Munising Avenue, Munising, MI 49862
www.northernwaters.com

Paddling Michigan 906-228-5447
321 South Lakeshore Blvd, Marquette, MI 49855
www.paddlingmichigan.com

MANISTIQUE RIVER

Big Cedar Campground & Canoe Livery 906-586-6684
7936 State Hwy. M-77, Germfask, MI 49836
http://www.bigcedarcampground.com/

Northland Outfitters 906-586-9801, 800-808-3FUN
8174 Hwy M-77, Germfask, MI 49836
http://www.northoutfitters.com/

U.P. Wide Adventure Guide 906-430-0547
W6508 Epoufette BayRoad, Naubinway, MI 49762
http://www.upwideadventureguide.com/

MENOMINEE RIVER

Northwoods Wilderness Outfitters 906-774-9009, 1-800-530-8859
N-4088 Pine Mountain Road, Iron Mountain, MI 49801
http://www.northwoodsoutfitters.com/

MICHIGAMME RIVER

Michi-Aho Resort 906-875-3514
2181 M-69, Crystal Falls, MI 49920
http://www.michiahoresort.com/

Northwoods Wilderness Outfitters 906-774-9009, 1-800-530-8859
N-4088 Pine Mountain Road, Iron Mountain, MI 49801
http://www.northwoodsoutfitters.com/

Uncle Ducky Outfitters 906-228-5447, 877-228-5447
434 E. Prospect, Marquette, MI 49855
http://www.uncleduckyoutfitters.com/

MILLECOQUINS RIVER

U.P. Wide Adventure Guide 906-430-0547
W6508 Epoufette BayRoad, Naubinway, MI 49762
http://www.upwideadventureguide.com/

ONTONAGON RIVER

Sylvania Outfitters, Inc. 906-358-4766
E23423 Hwy. 2, Watersmeet, MI 49969
http://www.sylvaniaoutfitters.com/

PAINT RIVER

Michi-Aho Resort 906-875-3514
2181 M-69, Crystal Falls, MI 49920
http://www.michiahoresort.com/

Northwoods Wilderness Outfitters 906-774-9009, 1-800-530-8859
N-4088 Pine Mountain Road, Iron Mountain, MI 49801
http://www.northwoodsoutfitters.com/

PINE RIVER

U.P. Wide Adventure Guide 906-430-0547
W6508 Epoufette BayRoad, Naubinway, MI 49762
http://www.upwideadventureguide.com/

STURGEON RIVER

Sturgeon River Canoe Livery 906-523-3523
40861 Sturgeon River Rd., Chassell, MI 49916

TAHQUAMEMON RIVER

Tahquamenon General Store Canoe & Kayak Rentals 906-429-3560
39991 W. Highway 123, Paradise, MI 49768

The Woods 906-203-7624
P.O. Box 536, Newberry, MI 49868
www.thewoodscanoerental.net

U.P. Wide Adventure Guide 906-430-0547
W6508 Epoufette BayRoad, Naubinway, MI 49762
http://www.upwideadventureguide.com/

TWO HEARTED RIVER

Two Hearted Canoe Trips, Inc. 906- 658-3357
32752 County Road 423, Newberry, MI 49868
http://www.rainbowlodgemi.com/

U.P. Wide Adventure Guide 906-430-0547
W6508 Epoufette BayRoad, Naubinway, MI 49762
http://www.upwideadventureguide.com/

AUSABLE RIVER

Alcona Canoe Rental & Campground 989-735-2973, 800-526-7080
6351 Bamfield Road, Glennie, MI 48737
http://www.alconacanoes.com/

Bear Paw Cabins & Canoe Livery 989-826-3313
3744 W. M72, Luzerne, MI 48636

Borcher's Ausable Canoe Livery 989-348-4921, 800-762-8756
101 Maple St., Grayling, MI 49738
http://www.canoeborchers.com/

Carlisle Canoes 989-348-2301
110 State St, Grayling, MI 49738
http://www.carlislecanoes.com/

Enchanted Acres Campground 231-266-5102
9581 N. Brooks Rd., Irons, MI 49644
http://www.enchantedacrescamp.com/

Gott's Landing 989-826-3411, 888-226-8748(Reservations only)
701 N. Morenci Rd., Mio, MI 48647
http://www.gottslanding.com/

Hinchman Acres 989-826-3267, 800-438-0203
702 N. M-33, P. O. Box 220, Mio, MI 48647
http://www.hinchman.com

Jim's Canoe (989) 348-3203
1706 Wakeley Bridge Rd., Grayling, MI 49738
http://www.jim'scanoe.com/

Oscoda Canoe Rental 989-739-9040
678 River Rd., Oscoda, MI 48750
http://www.oscodacanoe.com/

Parmalee Trading Post 989-826-3543
78 North Red Oak Road, Lewiston, MI 49756
www.parmaleetradingpost.net

Penrod's AuSable River Resort 888-467-4837, 989-348-2910
100 Maple St., Grayling, MI 49738
http://www.penrodscanoe.com/

Quinlan Island Canoe Livery
11724 Steckert Bridge Rd. Roscommon, MI 48653

Rainbow Resort 989-826-3423
731 Camp Ten Road, Mio, MI 48647
mailto:info@rainbowresortmio.com

Rollway Resort 989-728-3322
6160 Rollways Road, Hale, MI 48739
http://www.rollwayresort.com/

Watters Edge Canoe Livery 989-275-5568, 800-672-9968
10799 Dana Dr., Roscommon, MI 48653
http://www.wecl.8k.com/

AUSABLE, SOUTH BRANCH

Campbell's Canoeing 989-275-5810, 800-722-6633
1112 Lake St., Roscommon, MI 48653
http://www.canoeatcampbells.com/

Hiawatha Canoe Livery 888-515-5213, 989-275-5213
1113 Lake Street, Roscommon, MI 48653
http://www.canoehiawatha.com/

Jim's Canoe (989) 348-3203
1706 Wakeley Bridge Rd., Grayling, MI 49738
http://www.jim'scanoe.com/

Paddle Brave Canoe Livery & Campground 989-275-5273, 800-681-7092
10610 Steckert Bridge Rd., Roscommon, MI 48653
http://www.paddlebrave.com/

Parmalee Trading Post 989-826-3543
78 N. Red Oak Rd, Lewiston, MI 49756
Watters Edge Canoe Livery 989-275-5568, 800-672-9968
10799 Dana Dr., Roscommon, MI 48653
http://www.wecl.8k.com/

BEAR RIVER

Bear River Canoe Livery 231-347-9038, 231-838-4141
2517 McDougal, Petosky, MI 49770

BETSIE RIVER

Alvina's Canoe and Boat Rental 231-276-9514
6470 Betsie River Rd. S, Interlochen, MI 49643

Betsie River Canoes & Campground 231- 879-3850
13598 Lindy Rd./Highway 602, Thompsonville, MI 49683
http://www.brcanoesandcampground.com/

Crystal Adventures Lodging & Rentals 231-651-9648
17227 Vondra Road, Thompsonville, MI 49683
www.crystaladventures.com

Hanmer's Riverside Resort 231-882-7783
2251 Benzie Hwy, Benzonia, MI 49616
http://hanmers.com/

Vacation Trailer Park Inc. 231-882-5101
2080 Benzie Hwy., Benzonia, MI 49616
http://www.vacationtrailer.com/

BLACK RIVER (Bangor-South Haven)

Kayak Kayak 616-366-1146
321 Douglas Ave., Holland, MI 49424
www.kayak-kayak.com

BLACK RIVER (Northern Lower Pennisula)

Black River Canoe Outfitters/Ma & Pa's Country Store 989-733-8054
M33 & Hackett Lake Rd., Onaway, MI 49765

BOARDMAN RIVER

Lyf Motiv Adventures 231-944-1146
205 Garland St., Traverse City, MI 49684
www.lyfmotivadvs.com

Ranch Rudolf 231-947-9529
6841 Brown Bridge Rd., Traverse City, MI 49686
http://www.ranchrudolf.com/

CEDAR RIVER

Cedar River Canoe Trips 989-387-8658
12 East M61, Gladwin, MI 48624
www.gladwinboatrental.com

CHIPPEWA RIVER

Buckley's Mountainside Canoes 989-772-5437, 877-776-2800
4700 W. Remus Rd., Mt. Pleasant, MI 48858
http://www.buckleyscanoes.com/

Chippewa River Outfitters 989-772-5474, 888-775-6077
3763 S. Lincoln Rd., Mt Pleasant, MI 48858
http://www.chipoutfitters.com/

CLINTON RIVER

Clinton River Canoe & Kayak Rentals; Outdoor Escorts LLC 248-421-3445
916 Highlander, Lake Orion, MI 48362
www.outdoorescorts.com

COLDWATER RIVER

Indian Valley 616-891-8579
8200 108th, Middleville, MI 49333
http://www.indianvalleycampgroundandcanoe.com/

CRYSTAL RIVER

Crystal River Outfitters 231-334-4420
6249 W. River Rd., Glen Arbor, MI 49696
http://www.crystalriveroutfitters.com/

DOWAGIAC RIVER

Doe-Wah-Jack's Canoe Rental Inc. 888-782-7410, 269-782-7410
52963 M-51 N., Dowagiac, MI 49047
http://www.paddledcri.com/

FAWN RIVER

Liquid Therapy Canoe & Kayak Rentals 269-273-9000
221 S. Main St., Three Rivers, MI 49093
http://www.liquidtherapypaddling.com/

FLAT RIVER

Double R Ranch Resort 616-794-0520
4424 Whites Bridge Rd., Belding, MI 48809
http://www.doublerranch.com/

FLINT RIVER

Good Ol' Redbeard's General Store 810-210-7602
114 E. Main Street, Flushing, MI 48433

Pedals to Paddles 810-793-0000
4639 Water St, Columbiaville, MI 48421
http://www.pedalstopaddles.com/

GALIEN RIVER

Outpost Sports 269-637-5555
114 Dyckman, South Haven, MI 49090
www.outpostsports.com

GRAND RIVER

Grand Fish 517-410-0801
530 River Street, Lansing, MI 48933
www.thegrandfish.com

Grand Rogue Campground and Canoe 616-361-1053
6400 West River Dr., Belmont, MI 49306
http://www.grandrogue.com/

Kayak Kayak 616-366-1146
321 Douglas Ave., Holland, MI 49424
www.kayak-kayak.com

Lakeshore Kayak Rental 616-566-1325
Grand Haven, MI 49417
www.lakeshorekayakrental.com

Wacousta Canoe Livery 517-626-6873
9988 Riverside Drive, Eagle, MI 48822

HERSEY RIVER

Hersey Canoe Livery 231-832-7220
625 E. 4th St., Hersey, MI 49639
http://www.herseycanoe.com/

HURON RIVER

Argo Canoe Livery 734-794-6241
1055 Longshore Drive, Ann Arbor, MI 48105
www.a2gov.org/canoe

Gallup Canoe Livery 734-794-6240
3000 Fuller Road, Ann Arbor, MI 48105
www.a2gov.org/canoe

Heavner Canoe Rental 248-685-2379
2775 Garden Rd., Milford, MI 48381
http://www.heavnercanoe.com/

Skip's Huron River Canoe Livery 734-768-8686
3780 Delhi Ct., Ann Arbor, MI 48103

Village Canoe Rental 248-685-9207
1216 Garden, Milford, MI 48381
http://www.villagecanoerental.com/

JORDAN RIVER

Jordan Valley Outfitters 231-536-0006
311 N. Lake St. (M-66), East Jordan, MI 49727
http://www.jvoutfitters.com/

Swiss Hideaway, Inc 231-536-2341
1953 Graves Crossing, Mancelona, MI 49659
http://www.jordanriverfun.com/

KALAMAZOO RIVER

Kayak Kayak 616-366-1146
321 Douglas Ave., Holland, MI 49424
www.kayak-kayak.com

Old Allegan Canoe /Kayaker's Run 269-561-5481
2722 Old Allegan Rd, Fennville, MI 49408
http://www.oldallegancanoe.com/

Running Rivers Inc. 269-673-3698
Wade's Bayou Park, Douglas, MI 49406
www.running-rivers.com

Twin Pines Campground and Canoe Livery 517-524-6298
9800 Wheeler Rd., Hanover, MI 49241

LITTLE MANISTEE RIVER

Enchanted Acres Campground 231-266-5102
9581 N. Brooks Rd., Irons, MI 49644
http://www.enchantedacrescamp.com/

Pine Creek Canoe Livery 231-848-7170
13604 Caberfae Hwy., Wellston, MI 49689

LITTLE MUSKEGON RIVER

Bob & Pat's White Birch Canoe Trips & Campground 231-328-4547
Paradise Rd., Falmouth, MI 49632
http://www.whitebirchcanoe.com/

Wisner Rents Canoes 231-652-6743
25 W. Water St., Newaygo, MI 49337
http://www.wisnercanoes.com/

LOOKING GLASS RIVER

Wacousta Canoe Livery 517-626-6873
9988 Riverside Drive, Eagle, MI 48822

MANISTEE RIVER

Chippewa Landing 231-313-0832
10420 Chippewa Landing Trail, Manton, MI 49663
http://www.chippewalanding.com/

Enchanted Acres Campground 231-266-5102
9581 N. Brooks Rd., Irons, MI 49644
http://www.enchantedacrescamp.com/

Long's Canoe Livery 989-348-7224, 231-258-3452
8341 M-72 N.E., Kalkaska, MI 49646
http://www.longscanoelivery.com/

Missaukee Paddle Sports 231-839-8265
214 S. Main Street, Lake City, MI 49651
http://www.missaukeepaddlesports.com/

Pine Creek Lodge 231-848-4431
13544 Caberfae Hwy., Wellston, MI 49689
http://www.pinecreeklodge.net/

Pine River Paddlesports Center 231-862-3471
9590 Grand View Hwy. S37, Wellston, MI 49689
http://www.thepineriver.com/

Shel-Haven Canoe Rental 989-348-2158
P.O.Box 268, Grayling,MI 49738
http://www.shelhaven.com/

Smithville Landing 231-839-4579
M-66 on the Manistee River P.O.Box 341, Lake City, MI 49651
http://www.smithvillelanding.com/

Wilderness Canoe Trips 800-873-6379, 231-885-1485
6052 Riverview Rd., Mesick, MI 49668
http://www.wildernesscanoetripsonline.com/

MAPLE RIVER

Maple River Campground 989-981-6792
15420 French Rd., Pewamo, MI 48873
www.michcampgrounds.com/mapleriver

MUSKEGON RIVER

Bob & Pat's White Birch Canoe Trips & Campground 231-328-4547
Paradise Rd., Falmouth, MI 49632
http://www.whitebirchcanoe.com/

Chinook Campground 231-834-7505
5741 W. 112th, Grant, MI 49327
www.chinookcampground.com

Croton Dam Float Trips 231-952-6037
5355 Croton Road, Newaygo, MI 49337
http://wwofn.tripod.com/

Duggan's Canoe Livery 989-539-7149
3100 N. Temple Drive, Harrison, MI 48625

Hersey Canoe Livery 231-832-7220
625 E. 4th St., Hersey, MI 49639
http://www.herseycanoe.com/

Lakeshore Kayak Rental 616-566-1325
Grand Haven, MI 49417
www.lakeshorekayakrental.com

Missaukee Paddle Sports 231-839-8265
214 S. Main Street, Lake City, MI 49651
http://www.missaukeepaddlesports.com/

Muskegon River Camp & Canoe 231-734-3808 River Country Campground (New Name)
6281 River Rd., Evart, MI 49631
http://www.campandcanoe.com/

Mystery Creek Campground 231-652-6915
9570 S. Wisner, Newaygo, MI 49337
www.chinookcamping.com

Old Log Resort 231-743-2775
12062 M-115, Marion, MI 49665
http://www.oldlogresort.com/

River Rat Canoe Rental 231-834-9411
8702 River Dr. Bridgeton Twnshp, Grant, MI 49327
http://www.riverratcanoerental.com/

Salmon Run Campground & Vic's Canoes 231-834-5495
8845 Felch Ave., Grant, MI 49327
http://www.salmonrunmi.com/

Sawmill Tube and Canoe Livery 231-796-6408
230 Baldwin St., Big Rapids, MI 49307
http://www.sawmillmi.com/

Wisner Rents Canoes 231-652-6743
25 W. Water St., Newaygo, MI 49337
http://www.wisnercanoes.com/

OCQUEOC RIVER

Ocqueoc Outfitters 989-245-7204 or 989-734-4208
15524 US23 N at the Ocqueoc River, Ocqueoc, MI 49759
www.ocqueocoutfitters.com

PAW PAW RIVER

Paw Paw River Campgrounds & Canoes 269-463-5454
5355 Michigan Hwy 140, Watervliet, MI 49098
www.pawpawrivercampgroundandcanoes.com

PENTWATER RIVER

Pentwater River Outfitters 231-869-2999
42 W. 2nd Street, Pentwater, MI 49449
www.pentwaterriveroutfitters.com

PERE MARQUETTE RIVER

Baldwin Canoe Rental 231-745-4669, 800-272-3642
9117 South M37, P. O. Box 269, Baldwin, MI 49304
http://www.baldwincanoe.com/

Ivan's Canoe Rental 231-745-3361, 231-745-9345
7332 South M-37, Baldwin, MI 49304
http://www.ivanscanoe.com/

Pere Marquette Expeditions/Nelson's Frontier Market, 231-845-7285
1649 South Pere Marquette Hwy, Ludington, MI 49431
www.pmexpeditions.com

River Run Canoe Livery 231-757-2266
600 S Main St., Scottville, MI 49454
http://www.riverruncanoerental.com/

PIGEON RIVER (Northern-Lower Pennisula)

Big Bear Adventures 231-238-8181
4271 S. Straits Hwy., Indian River, MI 49749
http://www.bigbearadventures.com/

PIGEON RIVER (by Grand Haven))

Kayak Kayak 616-366-1146
321 Douglas Ave., Holland, MI 49424
www.kayak-kayak.com

Lakeshore Kayak Rental 616-566-1325
Grand Haven, MI 49417
www.lakeshorekayakrental.com

PIGEON RIVER (by Three Rivers)

Liquid Therapy Canoe & Kayak Rentals 269-273-9000
221 S. Main St., Three Rivers, MI 49093
http://www.liquidtherapypaddling.com/

PINEBOG RIVER

Tip-O-Thumb Canoe & Kayak Rental 989-738-7656
2475 Port Austin Rd., Port Austin, MI 48467

PINE RIVER

Enchanted Acres Campground 231-266-5102
9581 N. Brooks Rd., Irons, MI 49644
http://www.enchantedacrescamp.com/

Horina Canoe & Kayak Rental 231-862-3470
9889 M-37 South, Wellston, Michigan 49689
http://www.horinacanoe.com/

Pine River Paddlesports Center 231-862-3471
9590 Grand View Hwy. S37, Wellston, MI 49689
http://www.thepineriver.com/

Shlomer Canoes & Kayaks 231-862-3475
11390 N. M-37, Irons, MI 49644
http://www.shomlercanoes.com/

Sportsman's Port Canoes, Campground 231- 862-3571, 888-226-6301
10487 W. M55 Hwy., Wellston, MI 49689
http://www.sportsmansport.com/

Wilderness Canoe Trips 800-873-6379, 231-885-1485

6052 Riverview Rd., Mesick, MI 49668
http://www.wildernesscanoetripsonline.com/

PLATTE RIVER

Honor Canoe Rental 231-325-0112
2212 Valley Road/US-31, Honor, MI 49640
www.honorcanoerentals.com/

Riverside Canoes 231-325-5622
5042 Scenic Hwy., Honor, MI 49640
http://www.canoemichigan.com/

Trading Post 231-325-2202
8294 Deadstream Road, Honor, MI 49640
www.canoeplatteriver.com

PORTAGE RIVER & PRAIRIE RIVER

Liquid Therapy Canoe & Kayak Rentals 269-273-9000
221 S. Main St., Three Rivers, MI 49093
http://www.liquidtherapypaddling.com/

RED CEDAR RIVER

MSU Bikes 517-432-3400
B10 Bessey Hall, East Lansing, MI 48824
www.bikes.msu.edu/canoe-rentals.html

RIFLE RIVER

Big Mike's Canoe Rental 989-473-3444
2575 Rose City Rd., Lupton, MI 48635
http://www.canoe4rent.com/

Cedar Springs Campground, Canoe 989-654-3195
334 Melita Rd., Sterling, MI 48659

River View Campground & Canoe Livery 989-654-2447
5755 N. Town Line Rd., Sterling, MI 48659
http://www.riverviewcampground.com/

Russell Canoes & Campgrounds 989-653-2644
146 Carrington St., Omer, MI 48749
http://www.russellcanoe.com/

Troll Landing Campground & Canoe Livery 989-345-7260
2660 Rifle River Trail, West Branch, MI 48661
http://www.trolllanding.com/

White's Canoe Livery 989-654-2654
400 S. Melita, Sterling, MI 48659
http://www.whitescanoe.com/

Whispering Pines Campground & Canoe Livery 989-653-3321
538 S. Hale (M65), Twining, MI 48766-9715
www.whisperpines.com

RIVER RAISIN

River Raisin Canoe Livery 734-529-9029
1151 Plank Rd., Dundee, MI 48131
http://www.riverraisincanoelivery.com/

ROCKY RIVER

Liquid Therapy Canoe & Kayak Rentals Inc. 269-273-9000
221 S. Main St., Three River, MI 49093
http://www.liquidtherapypaddling.com/

ROGUE RIVER

AAA Canoe Rental 616-866-9264
525 Northland Dr., Rockford, MI 49341
http://www.aaacanoerental.com/

Grand Rogue Campground and Canoe 616-361-1053
6400 West River Dr., Belmont, MI 49306
www.grandrogue.com

ROUGE RIVER

Heavner Canoe Rental 248-685-2379
2775 Garden Rd., Milford, MI 48381
http://www.heavnercanoe.com

SHIAWASSEE RIVER

Fairbanks Canoes & Kayaks 810-287-9618
Linden MI
fairbankscanoesandkayaks@gmail.com

Walnut Hills Campgrounds, Canoe 989-634-9782
7685 Lehring Rd., Durand, MI 48429

ST. JOSEPH RIVER

Liquid Therapy Canoe & Kayak Rentals 269-273-9000
221 S. Main St., Three Rivers, MI 49093
http://www.liquidtherapypaddling.com/

Mendon Country Inn 800-304-3366 or 269-496-8132
440 W. Main Street, Mendon, MI 49072
www.mendoncountryinn.net

STURGEON RIVER
Beckwoods Canoe Rental 989-785-4081
12520 Airport Rd., Atlanta, MI 49709

Big Bear Adventures 231-238-8181
4271 S. Straits Hwy., Indian River, MI 49749
http://www.bigbearadventures.com/

Henley's Canoe & Kayak Rental 213-525-9994
13062 Rail Road St., Wolverine, MI 49799
http://www.henleysrentals.com

THORNAPPLE RIVER

Indian Valley 616-891-8579
8200 108th, Middleville, MI 49333
http://www.indianvalleycampgroundandcanoe.com/

U-Rent-Em Canoe Livery (269) 945-3191
805 W Apple St., Hastings, Michigan 49058
www.urentemcanoe.com

**Whispering Waters Campground and Canoes
269-945-5166**
1805 N. Irving Rd., Hastings, MI 49058
http://www.whisperingwatersonline.com/

THUNDER BAY RIVER

Beckwoods Canoe Livery 989-785-4081
12520 Airpot Rd., Atlanta, MI 49709

**Campers Cove Campground and Canoe 888-306-3708,
989-356-3708**
5005 Long Rapids Rd., Alpena, MI 49707
http://www.camperscovecampground.com/

Thunder Bay River Canoe & Kayak 989-785-2187
12520 Airport Rd., Atlanta, MI 49709
http://www.thunderbaycanoeing.com/

TITTABAWASSEE RIVER

Cedar River Canoe Trips 989-387-8658
12 East M61, Gladwin, MI 48624
www.gladwinboatrental.com

WHITE RIVER

Happy Mohawk Canoe Livery 231-894-4209
735 Fruitvale Rd., Montague, MI 49437
http://www.happymohawk.com/

Kellogg's Canoes 231-854-1415
P.O. Box 272, Hesperia, MI 49421
http://home1.gte.net/lkellogg/

Powers Outdoors 231-893-8107, 616-863-8107
4523 Dowling St., Mi 49437
http://www.powersoutdoors.com/

PADDLING & CAMPING CHECKLIST

bug spray/Vicks VapoRub (deer flies hate the smell)

plastic drop cloths (rain)   trash bags

dry (waterproof) bags   mosquito head net

water & food   sunblock

forks & plates   music

nose strips (for our loud friends)   ear plugs (see nose strips)

reynolds wrap (grub leftover)   small pillow

small & large ziplocks   first aid kit*

tent/sleeping bag   life jacket

knife   clothesline rope

pots/pans/large spoon   grill/grate

fire starter/matches   blankets

2 sets of keys   river shoes/dry shoes

Thermarest/air mattress   river & dry clothes

bungee cords   cooler, ice, water

frisbees   campsite chairs

rain poncho   flashlights

towel   soap, toothpaste/brush

toilet paper   euchre decks

```
can opener                      camera

brimmed hat                     $$$ & wallet

handtowel/paper plates          sunglasses


* the first aid kit contents: bandages, adhesive tape, aspirin,
  antiseptic wipes, antibiotic ointment/Neosporin
```

About the Author

Doc Fletcher shares his love of canoeing and kayaking with readers in his 4th book, *Paddling Michigan's Hidden Beauty: The Rivers, The Towns, The Taverns*.

Doc has also authored:
Weekend Canoeing in Michigan
Michigan Rivers Less Paddled
Canoeing and Kayaking Wisconsin

A life-long resident of Michigan, he attended Eastern Michigan University where, in order of importance (1) he met his wife Maggie and (2) graduated in 1976 with a Bachelor's Degree in Marketing.

In 1981, Maggie and Doc were married along the banks of the Huron River in Ypsilanti. They are shown above on their wedding day with Doc's Mom and Dad, Mary and Herb.

Visit Doc's website at www.canoeingmichiganrivers.com